Monday Morning
PREACHER

Things I Wish I Had Known as a Young Pastor

Roger Loomis

ISBN 978-1-63903-435-2 (paperback)
ISBN 978-1-63903-436-9 (digital)

Christian Faith Publishing
832 Park Avenue
Meadville, PA 16335
www.christianfaithpublishing.com

Printed in the United States of America

Nothing on earth matches the wonders of the local church! What can pastors do to stem the tide of Christians who see regular attendance as optional?

Dear Reader,

*S*ome of Jesus's greatest ministry took place in obscurity. Recall his night encounter with Nicodemus and his conversation with the woman at the well. Both were life-changing discourses. Similarly, most of what pastors encounter today also takes place behind the scenes. Pulpit ministry counts for approximately 12 percent of their weekly schedule. For many pastors, too many of their remaining hours are spent doing damage control. Yes, the devil is the local church's most formidable enemy. Yes, American culture is becoming noticeably more antagonistic toward Christianity. However, a lot of church problems develop from within. Current church fallout supports this unfortunate reality.

Drawing from forty-three years of pastoral ministry, *Monday Morning Preacher* submits forty potential reasons for the many back-door exits. Pastors must ask themselves, "Is my church healthy?" "Am I healthy—spiritually, mentally, emotionally, and physically?" "Am I willing to be misunderstood?" "Do I feel compelled to be loved and accepted by everyone?" "How well do I handle conflict?" "Is my success measured by crowds and offerings?" "Does my church need to rethink its ministry approach?"

Honest answers to these questions and others could mean the difference between having a growing church or a compromised future. Understanding these forty observations may ensure your church's perpetuity. *Monday Morning Preacher* sounds a clarion call for believers everywhere to stem the tide of declining attendance.

Christ-honoring local churches are God's gift to every community. May the Holy Spirit rekindle a desire in the hearts of true Christians everywhere and renew their passion for God's house, the local church.

Dedication

I have pastored hundreds of people over the years, and many have impacted my life in ways too numerous to mention. A telephone call in January 2014 fastened my heart to yet another special man. Eventually, I became his pastor. "Is this Pastor Roger?" he asked. "This is Freddie Grupe, and I attended your church on Sunday..."

After forty-five minutes of discussing my theology and ideas about what the Christian life should look like, this wonderful man of grace endeared himself to my heart like few have. Fred grew up under legalistic preaching, later coached girls' basketball, played bass in a rock 'n' roll band and held Thursday evening Bible studies in his home for many years. He believed strongly in the Gospel of grace and to quote him directly, "I don't give a 'rat's Ashtabula' how anyone feels about my animosity toward any Gospel message that hurts people or causes them to live in bondage."

Fred was given up to die almost twenty years before he actually passed away in August 2018. That wonderful heart quit beating after four years of attending Hope Community Church in Jefferson, Ohio. During his time with us, I witnessed the beauty of "real Christianity." Fred struggled with heart disease but filled his days sharing his unique brand of humor and heartfelt love for God and His people. And I cried when he died. His life intersected with mine, showing me great respect and the desire to further embrace God's Word. He called me Captain.

After Fred landed at Hope Community, he always arrived early and was one of the last ones to leave. Hope was blessed to have him and heaven was honored to welcome him. I thank God for our local church, which brought Fred, me, and several others into a special relationship. Freddie G, I can't wait to hear your corny jokes again and your update on how the local church impacted your life.

Miss you, Fred.

Pastor Roger Loomis

Contents

Introduction

Monday Morning Preacher represents a composite of forty-three years of pastoral ministry that explores behind-the-scenes reasons church attendance continues to decline in America. Many blame it on Satan's relentless assaults, as he is the Church's most formidable enemy. Others point toward a growing anti-Christian sentiment in American culture. Admittedly, both interrelate. However, I believe the answers to much church decline—and solutions—can be found within churches themselves. I am a Christian pragmatist, one who recognizes symptoms, then searches out root causes. In this book, I identify forty potential issues that arise in every contemporary evangelical church at some point. Simultaneously, I insert biblical principles to bring solutions. My favorite people are pastors, and I have a heart to help them succeed in their most noble calling.

According to a new study from the Hartford Institute for Religious Research, most American churches now have less than one hundred in weekend attendance. In 2005, the median attendance was 129. That fell to 105 in 2010 and down to eighty this past year—COVID-19 notwithstanding. This means half of all American churches have a weekend attendance of eighty or less. Even the rise of megachurches has not stemmed the tide of overall decline. Currently, 1,500 megachurches, defined by the Hartford Institute as those Protestant churches having two thousand or more people in average weekend attendance, and totaling three million aggregate attendance, still represent a miniscule segment of the United States population. Research also indicates that the average tenure for pastors in the American Church is four years. Those in youth ministry average two years! Finally, Pastoral Care Inc. indicates that 250 evangelical pastors leave the ministry each month. Some estimates go as high as 1,500 monthly. Pastoral Care Inc. is an organization designed to help support ministers through research, educational support, and providing immediate assistance. At any rate, the numbers are sobering. One is too many! Accelerated ministry turnover is definitely a cause for concern.

Why the drop in attendance? And why are so many pastors stepping down from church ministry altogether? It's time to ask the hard questions. This challenge I willingly accept. In retrospect, I ask myself, "How could I have better prepared for the ministry challenges I faced?" To be informed is to be both prepared and armed. My sincere desire is that pastors everywhere learn from my mistakes and successes in order to sidestep any potential church setbacks. I'm not a self-made martyr, just a fellow pastor who wants to see you and your church reach its highest potential. Most of my observations relate to churches of less than two hundred in attendance. However, any leader can benefit from the information presented.

Over the years, when asked where I received my ministry training, I jokingly responded, "God's School of Hard Knocks." And truthfully, I wasn't kidding. As much as I enjoyed my Bible classes at Evangel University, I have to admit the classroom did not—could not—completely prepare me for local church leadership. Occasionally making the dean's list never guaranteed my ability to successfully navigate difficult situations that threatened church unity and caused people to leave. Some things can only be learned through on-the-job training. Still, how many difficult challenges could have been avoided had I known then what I know now? Like me, other aspiring men and women left Bible colleges and seminaries full of vision and an overwhelming desire to win the lost to Christ. Our intentions were compassion-driven and our hearts yearned to preach the Word of God and be the best leaders possible.

Then, reality hit! We discovered that while the classroom prepared us "to rightfully divide the Word" (2 Tim. 2:15), nothing could prepare us to handle carnal Christians, critics, control freaks, those with poor people skills, gossips, religious spirits, family issues, unreasonable positional leaders, a pandemic, and a multitude of other unfortunate scenarios that characterize contemporary ministry. And given time, many wonderful leaders found themselves sidelined in a quagmire of gross misunderstandings, unkind words, harsh accusations, and a lot of unfair circumstances that threatened to jeopardize their influence and, at times, even their sanity. I specifically found myself torn by people who were self-serving. After particularly hard weeks, I was tempted to call it quits.

Herein, I present information that pertains to both the pew and the pulpit. The correlations expose sad realities. Perhaps we can stem the unfortunate tide of church fallout by exposing both the tactics of the enemy and the carnal nature. It's hard work raising pastors! For obvious reasons, I could not have written this book until now. As previously stated, on-the-job training was both my instructor and, at times, my nemesis!

My wife and I planted a church in rural northeastern Ohio in 2017. And God has given us much favor in this village, population approximately three thousand. However, we have seen many people come and go. And most (nearly all) of them left without the courtesy of a sit-down conversation. A few left antagonistically—sending vague, even unkind texts or hurtful letters.

How many former pastors, now in the secular marketplace, fight rejection, anger, even bitterness, along with a sense of failure? I'm sure the numbers are staggering. I also wrote *Monday Morning Preacher* to remind anyone in this situation that you are not alone. There is purposeful life and kingdom productivity beyond formal ministry. God still loves you, and you are not a second-class Christian. You are not a failure! A failure is defined as someone who, after getting knocked down, refused to get back up. That's not you! Don't let anyone tell you otherwise.

I resigned pastoral ministry in 2012 to become a hospice chaplain. The gifts inside me transferred to one-on-one ministry instead of preaching to crowds. I love using my gifts to help individuals transition from this life to the next. God was not mad because I temporarily left the pastorate. His intention regardless was that I continued to point others to Christ.

I don't have all the answers, but hopefully, four decades of pastoring give me credibility to provide helpful insights for my brothers and sisters everywhere who have, in the past, or currently are struggling with individuals exiting their church doors for the last time. And for precious former pastors who feel both rejection and dejection.

At any rate, my intention is to openly confront the reasons people left every church I served. Oh, how I struggled with most every exit! Notice I said "most." In retrospect, some who departed needed to! Their staying would have been counterproductive to the overall forward movement of the church. However, most left unexpectedly and without saying goodbye. Speculations ran high! So what you hold is a collection of those speculations, all with a didactic edge. Pastors and other church leaders, be encouraged. You are responsible for delivering the message. Those in your charge are responsible for their reactions and subsequent decisions. Don't automatically assume blame for departures. God wants you to be the best you can be, and if you keep a pure, teachable heart, he will show you areas where you perhaps contributed to misunderstandings. After all, pastors, too, are people, subject to all the flaws and weaknesses of the flesh. But please don't allow the enemy to bring condemnation. Learn from your mistakes and move into your future by God's grace.

Monday Morning Preacher is a must read for all the unsung heroes who currently lead local churches and for those who led in the past. Like Monday morning quarterbacks, who review their post-game strategies, pastors need to perhaps revisit their Sunday service on Monday morning to celebrate their wins and to identify potential in-house issues that need wise and righteous attention. It is the behind-the-scenes issues that drain pastors of precious time and energy because they require constant monitoring. Each chapter is scaled back so that all who lead in today's church can more easily become aware of and act upon these observations.

The calling and responsibilities of a pastor come with great accountability. Let me explain. A lot of what happens in day-to-day ministry cannot be revealed or even discussed. People count on the confidentiality of wise, caring shepherds. To publicly discuss the idiosyncrasies of church life is to risk being misunderstood and create further problems. The enemy loves to publicly download church drama. Preach the "unsearchable riches of Christ" (Eph. 3:8) from your pulpit and deal with the other stuff in private.

During my third pastorate, I allowed hurtful individuals and church leaders to get under my skin. Instead of righteously processing my pain, I used the pulpit to vent my anger. How I regret this time in my ministry, but God in his mercy forgave and redirected me. My dear pastors, such rantings are never life-giving and always counterproductive to local church health. Please, please, please don't fall prey to this temptation.

I submit *Monday Morning Preacher* with a heart full of love for all the men and women who lead local churches. May you experience the favor of the Lord!

Part 1

This first section presents a backdrop of information to help the reader appreciate the biblical, theological, and historical support for the local church's right to exist and wonderful ability to impact our nation and local communities. Local churches are families of believers who gather in recognized meeting places to perpetuate the Gospel of Jesus Christ.

They comprise imperfect people who completely depend on God's grace to live in a manner pleasing to the Lord. Local churches remain earth's greatest venue to win the lost and disciple believers. Pastors must protect them from adverse influences, especially from within. They need to be aware of the many behind-the-scenes challenges that, when left unchecked, threaten to unwrap their church's future potential.

The author issues a clarion call for Christians to renew their passion to regularly gather together and to remember that while local churches may have their ups and downs, they still remain one of God's greatest gifts to every community. Heaven will be largely populated because of pastors and others who faithfully preached the life-changing Gospel of Jesus Christ. The author begs you to find a local faith community where you will experience life's more significant moments—good and bad—and find others to come alongside you. I'm just going to say it. Nothing, and I mean nothing on earth matches the wonders of the local church!

1

The Big Question

$\mathcal{I}$ love the local church. And I don't understand why so many Christians fail to share my enthusiasm. I am both a Christian and a pastor today because of a local church. I shudder to think where my life would have taken me without the influence of that wonderful group of people. So why are more and more believers in Christ treating regular church attendance as optional in their life?

Over 120 years ago, William Booth, founder of the Salvation Army, prophesied, "The chief danger of the twentieth century will be religion without the Holy Spirit, Christianity without Christ, forgiveness without repentance, salvation without regeneration, politics without God and heaven without hell." As I look back over my life and ministry, I have watched his words accurately and progressively unfold. And nowhere, in my opinion, do we see the fallout more obvious than in local churches. I further believe that Christians would do well to heed the words of the apostle Paul found in Ephesians 5:14: "Awake, sleeper, and arise from the dead, and Christ will shine on you." It's time for true believers to rekindle their love for the house of God. We live in a pivotal time in redemptive history and souls hang in the balance. While there may perhaps be much wrong with local church ministry, there's much more that's right! This I believe!

During the past four decades, it has been my honor to lead six churches in three states. Sadly, a common thread in all six has been the unfaithful attendance of many. A hit-and-miss attitude pervaded each one. Another thread, sadder still, was the fact that once individuals started treating regular weekly church attendance with a nonchalant attitude, they eventually dropped out altogether.

After my conversion in 1970, I wanted nothing else than to spend my life in and through the local church. My pastoral journey has introduced me to some of earth's most wonderful people. I have crossed paths with some of God's choicest saints who have impacted me in ways too numerous to count. The collective me is a result of those interactions. To be sure, I have experienced times of sadness, betrayal, tragedy, anger, and all the emotions that accompany rubbing elbows with people. However, I'm still one of the local church's biggest fans! In my mind, nothing on earth matches the wonder of Christ-honoring churches. Everything else pales in comparison. Putting carnal Christians, long-winded preachers, less-than-quality music, appeals for money, dress codes, the abuse of spiritual gifts, and more aside, I find nothing in life that impacts me like the local church. I've said it for years: "The church at its worst is better than the world at its best!"

I've sat in services where the piano playing sounded like it came out of Gunsmoke's famed Long Branch Saloon in Dodge City! You baby boomers know what I'm talking about! I've also been in services where the music sounded like the Cleveland Orchestra. None of this mattered, as pure hearts raised glorious harmony to heaven! I've been taught by the learned and unlearned. I've met hypocrites, egocentric pastors, critics—Negative Nellie and Gloomy Gus, along with David and Debbie Downer—and other "makes and models"; and my mind is still made up. You can't talk me out of it. The local church remains earth's greatest asset.

But I'm in a quandary. And I have a question that begs a response. Why do people leave local churches? *Why?* Again I ask, "W-h-h-y-y?" This unfortunate reality has bothered me to the point of pacing the floor at night. Introspection kicked in, and I asked myself, "What did I do?" "What didn't I do?" "Where did I go wrong?" A thousand questions came pouring into my mind. No answers. Only questions! I needed answers. That's why I was compelled to write this book. I thank God for the wonderful pastors-shepherds He placed in my life. I watched them also agonize over this issue. I watched them weep over the lost, visit the sick, preach, pray, prophesy, laugh, and perform the countless other tasks associated with local church ministry. And I saw the pained looks on their faces when people left their churches. I saw discouragement smother them like the coronavirus. I felt helpless to encourage them.

That is how *Monday Morning Preacher* was born. I have asked the hard questions, given this subject hours of contemplation, and now it's time to submit my thoughts to thousands of pastors, former pastors, and church leaders around this country and the world. And I believe I've hit on honest, long-awaited answers. And most of all, I hope, my pastor friends, that you quit being so hard on yourself the next time somebody leaves your church. There's a big chance that you will have nothing to do with it! Read on!

After each chapter, I ask several questions for you to ponder. These questions either reiterate the previously read material, or call on you to give further thought to the content presented.

Questions to Ponder

1. What is your reaction to William Booth's quote?

2. Why do you think a lot of Christians treat regular church attendance as optional in their life?

3. "The church at its worst is better than the world at its best." Do you agree? Why or why not?

4. Have you ever left a local church? Do you remember why? What did you learn from your experience?

2

Pastors Are People Too

For the most part, I have been loved by the people I served. A lot of wonderful individuals endeared themselves to me and my family. They knew we were imperfect but supported us anyway. They knew we were people too! Most understood that we lived in a glass house but remained unwilling to throw rocks. They loved unconditionally, not placing unreasonable expectations on us.

The hugs, handshakes, dinner invitations, home visits, hospital visits, funerals, weddings, counseling sessions, and so much more, conjure up precious times and smiles. Memories of those now in heaven cause me to fight back tears when I recall our times together. They are among the "great cloud of witnesses" (Heb. 12:1) that fill heaven's grandstand, awaiting the arrival of those on earth with whom they shared fellowship through a local church. How I miss them! Those times of rich, deep personal interaction made ministry fulfilling and special. We pastors are a privileged group.

Most of all, I think about the many who responded to the preaching of God's Word. I remember the tears, the decisions to repent, to make life changes, and the faces of those who came forward during altar invitations to give their lives to Jesus Christ. Some are in ministry today—missionaries, pastors, pastor's wives, and other leaders. These are the people I choose to remember as I stroll down memory lane. They are success stories—not mine, but the Lord's. I was privileged to be in the moment. My heart still overflows with gratitude. No pastor will fully realize the scope of lives touched until he or she participates in "heaven's roundup." Consider Paul's words to Timothy regarding pastoral rewards: "Henceforth there is laid up for me the crown of righteousness, which the Lord, the righteous Judge, will award to me on that day" (2 Tim. 4:8). I choose to keep my eye on the prize, not the problem people!

Did I say "problem people"? All pastors deal with people who bring stress and pain into their lives, people who place unreasonable demands and expectations on them. My saving grace has been to remember that Jesus died for them too! In the meantime, we pastors all have our war stories to tell.

Pastor friend, allow me to be blunt. Other pastors usually don't want to hear your stories. They really don't! I believe it's because they struggle with their own pain and our stories only compound their personal misery. I even had a pastor tell me over breakfast that he was going to leave if I didn't quit rehearsing my pain. Obviously, he hurt my feelings; however, later I realized that all pastors share similar pain, and to hear about the pain others are experiencing may put them on emotional overload. Admittedly, pain not processed redemptively can drive pastors to focus inwardly and become self-centered. We succumb to a victim mentality if we allow it. After all, my pain is just as real as the next guys! Later, you will read about people who become "projects." I, too, have spent valuable time sharing my often-rehearsed stories with individuals who I'm sure felt like running away! And for that, I'm embarrassed and sorry.

Then, on the other hand, storytelling also has a righteous purpose; Jesus was a master storyteller, and he used stories to expose an issue and then to bring a resolve. I tell several ministry-related stories to illustrate my point and then to say, "Yes, this actually took place, but these things no longer define who I am." I present them as a point of discussion, not as open wounds that I continue to nurse. Otherwise, I have decided to place them under the blood of Jesus! We are called to share our victories not our defeats. We are victors, not victims! Right? Many years ago, I heard someone say, "Write your hurts in dust and your benefits in marble." Constantly weighing in on our own pain keeps us from being genuine toward the needs of others.

In addition, I've noticed something about Christians in general. Often, they fail to be truly compassionate. Let me ask you, "Have you ever been guilty of formulating in your mind what you're going to say next when someone is pouring out his heart to you?" Truthfully, I have! It's almost like we need to "one up the score." May God help us become better listeners, genuinely concerned and more apt to care about the needs of others than even our own. It's no accident we were created with two ears and one mouth! Ironically, pastors can become unfeeling toward people—a sad reality. But perhaps the reason is because we get hurt by the very people we are called to serve, and that pain lessens our ability to be real. In other words, we pull back emotionally. Insecurity rules!

In all six of my churches, I've encountered at least one—usually more than one—verbal ambush. Each time the perpetrator was swift and mean-spirited. Both men and women sought to put me in my place. Some were cowards who snail-mailed unsigned, typed letters. They had no respect for me or the position I held. And after each occasion, I felt vulnerable. The enemy downloaded his dastardly deeds using a broken, unfeeling Christian to thwart my leadership. Later, he tried to make me believe I was the only pastor ever to be confronted in such a manner. And after each assault, I was tempted to give up.

I still don't understand how people can address a pastor in such a way. Have they no fear of God? To be sure, my experiences were uniquely mine, and like you, I have been called to righteously process the pain of unrighteous encounters. During those times, the Lord called me into his "secret place" where I found consolation. "You hide [me] in the secret place of Your presence from the conspiracies of man; You keep [me] secretly in a shelter from the strife of tongues" (Ps. 31:20). He proved to be my burden-bearer. There, he taught me, offered me full pardon, and reminded me that I was precious to him; and that my performance in ministry would be judged, not on what I did wrong, or how I was treated, but on my heart's condition and according to my faithfulness.

The Lord always looks at the motivations of the heart. Pure hearts and motives strive to maintain godly relationships. This fact prompts me to discuss the coming judgment when all believers will individually stand before the Lord to give an account for "deeds done while in their body" (2 Cor. 5:10). How should the reality of this coming judgment affect how we interact with others during our time on earth? Let's see.

Questions to Ponder

1. If you're a pastor, take time right now to think about the many people you have known. What specific memories come to mind?

2. The author suggests that pastors live in glass houses. What are the implications behind this statement?

3. Why do some pastors become poor listeners?

4. Why is it important for pastors to righteously process their unrighteous encounters?

3

When It's All Said and Done

$\mathcal{I}$ have long wondered how the judgment seat of Christ will factor into my pastoral performance. I believe heaven will right all wrongs, and that one day I will stand before the Lord for a private evaluation. What will be the purpose of this one-on-one encounter? Theologians refer to this as the bema judgment, taken from the Greek word for "a raised platform from which to judge."

First, this judgment will not concern our sins. Our sins were judged on the Cross and placed under the precious blood of Jesus. We will be in heaven because we placed our faith in the atoning blood of Christ. Eternal life will be our prize and heaven our home. This, my friend, is the Gospel!

Second, know with certainty this judgment will not be conducted to determine our value or worth to God. Jesus proved our value when he gave his life on the Cross. It may be a cliche, but I agree: "The ground at the foot of the Cross is level and we all find the same favor and forgiveness." Our sins will not be placed on a continuum, with ten being the highest score. Rather, the blood of Jesus forgives all sin. We often are guilty of comparing our sin with murderers and other heinous offenders; however, when it comes to sin, we all "fall short" (Rom. 3:23). At the judgment bar of God we will stand, not convicted but cleansed. We will not face future condemnation. Thank you, Jesus!

At the judgment seat of Christ, we will not be judged on the magnitude of our earthly assignment but on our resolve to be faithful. We want to hear Jesus say, "Well done good and *faithful* servant" (Matt. 25:23). Pastors of large churches will not be elevated above those of smaller churches. We will stand in line with Billy Graham and other Gospel greats! This judgment will be based on qualitative principle, not quantitative. The answer to the following question will mean everything: Were we faithful to complete what the Lord gave us to do? Crowd size will not be the determining factor.

Remember, if we know Christ, our salvation will already be assured. We'll stand before God, not to be judged for our salvation; instead we will be rewarded for our good deeds, and we may suffer loss. Not loss of eternal security, but loss of rewards. "We must all appear before the judgment seat of Christ, that each one may receive what is due him for the things done while in the body, whether good or bad" (2 Cor. 5:10). These are sobering words indeed!

While the judgment seat of Christ will not be punitive in purpose, I believe there will be both rewards and loss of rewards. Let me explain. Paul writes, "Those things done while in the body." We are "body" people. We have a spirit and a soul that are housed within a body. Expressions of the spirit and soul are manifested through the body. In other words, when we look at people, we look at bodies. We don't see spirits and souls; we see a body. We discern spirits, but we don't "see" them." We relate to bodies. That's why God sent Jesus to us in the form of a baby. We are body people who caudle newborns! The writer to the Hebrews said, "Therefore, when He comes into the world, He says…'BUT A BODY YOU HAVE PREPARED FOR ME'" (10:5).

Bodies move as directed by the spirit and soul. Our mind-brain mechanism is a fascinating study! I'm not trying to sound spooky; I'm trying to put the bema judgment in a scriptural context. I firmly believe the primary topic of conversation between the Lord and us will be about our relationships on earth, specifically our broken relationships. Other sins done while in the body seem to be yet another emphasis in the whole of Scripture. "Those things done in secret" fall opposite to relationships that disintegrate for all to see. Luke 8:17 reminds us that "nothing is hidden that will not become evident, nor anything secret that will not be known and come to light."

The Scriptures indicate that words reveal our character. "For the mouth speaks out of that which fills the heart" (Matt. 12:34b). Another aspect of the bema judgment will involve "idle words." Jesus says, "But I tell you that every careless word that people speak, they shall give an accounting for it on the day of judgment. For by your words you will be justified, and by your words you will be condemned" (Matt. 36–37). Jesus refers to broken relationships that result from hurtful words spoken in haste, or perhaps in anger.

Can I be totally honest? All of us leave a trail of broken relationships as we navigate this life. Some leave behind more bodies than others! The Bible refers to these broken relationships as trespasses. It's no small wonder that Jesus taught his disciples to pray, "Forgive us our trespasses as we forgive those who trespass against us" (Matt. 6:12 NMB).

Sins against the body—sexual sins—are definitely potential concerns, but I think the wider spectrum of "things done while in the body" falls in the category of confessed sins that make heaven possible in the first place. "If we confess our sins, he is faithful and just to forgive us" (1 John 1:9). However, relationship issues that go unresolved in this life seem to be the highlighted concern in this verse.

Like you, I cannot say that all my experiences with people have been positive. I, too, have left behind a trail of damaged relationships. After forty-three years of full-time ministry, I can say with a degree of certainty that Christians many times fail miserably in the "relationship department." Much reproach is brought upon the Gospel when relationships turn sour. When Mahatma Gandhi, former prime minister of India, was asked why he did not accept Christianity, he replied, "I like your Christ. I do not like your Christians. Your Christians are so unlike your Christ." How sad! I still contend that the acid test of our faith is the way we treat others. The Bible obviously has much to say about relationships. As a matter of fact, it is a book about relationships—with God and others. Much attention is devoted to topics like forgiveness, our words, attitudes, and motives.

Let's continue to explore the meaning behind *trespasses*. Occasionally, we see signs that read "No Trespassing" posted on abandoned buildings, dilapidated homes, and fence posts. The dictionary defines this word as "a forcible or hostile entrance into the territory or rights of others." So why would Jesus use the word *trespasses* in this model prayer? How does it apply to relationships? Not many today use the word *trespasses* unless they adhere strictly to the *King James* language. Notice, however, that Jesus uses the word in the plural sense. I don't like what that suggests, do you?

To trespass means to go somewhere that's off limits, to go beyond preestablished boundaries. It also carries the negative connotation of debt: "Forgive us our debts as we forgive our debtors." In other words, we owe something in the sense of relationship failure. Matthew 6:12 uses the word *trespass* or *debt* (you choose!) to describe one who is under obligation. The strong implication is that those under obligation need to make amends where they have caused relationship damage. In Matthew 23:18, the word is used to describe one who is guilty of a wrong done and therefore, under obligation to make amends for misdeeds done. "Whoever swears by the altar is nothing, but whoever swears by the offering on it, he is obligated."

James 5:16 tells us to "confess our sins one to another that we may be healed." The word *sin* is taken from the Greek word *hamartias* and is better translated "faults." Perhaps we need to better understand the seriousness of this relationship dynamic. We live in a throwaway culture. Much of our food is packaged in disposable containers. New mothers appreciate the convenience of disposable diapers. Picnickers enjoy paper cups, plates, and other table wares. We also live in a self-centered culture that extols convenience over commitment. We are often obligated to no one, unless there's something in it for us. Many leave churches all too easily when their expectations are skewed.

A 2010 survey of one thousand church attenders asked the question, "Why does the church exist?" According to 89 percent polled, the church's purpose was "to take care of my family's needs and my spiritual needs." Only 11 percent said the purpose of the church is "to win the world for Jesus Christ." The "Me Generation" is speaking loudly! Many are all too willing to throw away their relationships in the church at the first sign of trouble. Let's be honest. Maintaining relationships requires hard work. Our no-fault divorce settlements are indicative of a culture that minimizes personal accountability for actions taken and words spoken. The acknowledgment of sin where one has wronged another is no longer a foregone conclusion. However, the Bible clearly teaches that we are under obligation to forgive the faults of others and to take whatever steps are necessary to maintain ongoing healthy relationships.

I'm thinking that many Christians understand the bema judgment in positive terms only. However, I submit that heads will hang low when Jesus inquires about relationships that were never mended in this life. This will not be a salvation issue but a reward-or-loss issue. Yes, there will be rewards for faithfulness, but remember, too, we will suffer loss for forgiveness that was never extended and for relationships that were never reconciled while on earth.

First Corinthians 3:13–15 reminds us,

> Every man's work will be made manifest: for the day shall declare it, because it shall be revealed by fire; and the fire shall try every man's work, of what sort it is. If any man's work abides which has built thereupon, he shall receive a reward. If any man's work shall be burned, he shall suffer loss: but he himself shall be saved, yet so as by fire.

The *New Living Translation* perhaps brings greater clarity to these verses:

> But there is going to come a time of testing at the judgment day to see what kind of work each builder has done. Everyone's work will be put through the fire to see whether or not it keeps its value. If the work survives the fire, that builder will receive a reward. But if the work is burned up, the builder will suffer great loss. The builders themselves will be saved, but like someone escaping through a wall of flames.

What kind of builder are you?

Let me requote Matthew 12:36. "But I tell you that men will have to give an account on the day of judgment for every careless word they have spoken. For by your words you will be acquitted, and by your words you will be condemned." Our tongue may be one of our body's smallest members, but it can be used to heal or kill relationships. Again, Jesus reminds us in Matthew 12:34, "For out of the abundance of the heart, the mouth speaks." What we say reveals what's inside our heart.

Conversely, soured relationships made sweet again will never be mentioned at the bema judgment. "If we confess our sin, He is faithful to forgive" (1 John 1:9a). Confessed sin, followed by repentance, is forgotten sin because of the blood of Jesus!

Yes, pastors are people too. We're all hopelessly flawed apart from the grace of God. Relationship breakdowns in the local church need not cause us separation in this life. Such fallout is unnecessary if we practice living life God's way. All of us need to work hard to ensure against potential loss in this life and the one to come. I see it this way: God places us in a local church and gives us opportunities to practice our faith, so we better know how to navigate our sphere of influence during the week. The house of God then becomes a safe zone where we learn how "to make right any wrongs done"! We've often heard it said, "This life is but a dress rehearsal for eternity." Let's determine to bring down the house!

Questions to Ponder

1. What are some of your favorite memories when you think about your former and current pastors?

2. Read 2 Timothy 4:8 again. What special reward does Paul say pastors will receive?

3. Constantly reliving our past hurts is not healthy? Why?

4. Referring to the judgment seat of Christ (bema judgment), what does "things done while in the body" refer to?

5. Do you have any broken relationships in your life that need to be reconciled? Perhaps a phone call, text, email, or a letter may be in order!

4

Never the Same Again

COVID-19 has forever changed our lives. The "normal" we once took for granted is gone. The year 2020, and now 2021, has altered our daily lives and challenged our priorities. My sphere of work and influence centers around the local church. As a church planter, I have witnessed the virus's negative impact, both locally and elsewhere. Churches, large and small, have experienced a decline in attendance. Mandatory quarantines, social distancing, masks, and the uncertainty of how or when the virus might spread has struck fear in the hearts of many. However, the purpose of this book is not to wax eloquent regarding the coronavirus. I'll let the medical professionals and historians weigh in regarding the overall impact of this worldwide plague.

Suffice it to say, people left churches long before the pandemic made its debut on the American stage in March 2020.

However, it may be entirely possible that a significant number of former churchgoers used the virus as an excuse to jump ship. Those on the periphery of local church life did not need a lot to persuade their exit. I believe this to be true. I have pastored six churches. And in all of them, people came and then left with regularity, never to be heard from again. This has been my sad reality. In retrospect, I automatically assumed the blame for peoples' decision to leave. Each time someone left, the enemy had a field day, as he is the "accuser of the brethren" (Rev. 12:10). I inadvertently assumed total responsibility for these decisions and with each departure became more and more inwardly distraught.

In retrospect, I can say that I maintained a pure heart and walked in integrity before the Lord. Was I perfect? Of course not! Did I make mistakes or lack sound judgment at times? You know I did! However, I can say with assurance that one day l will hear the Lord say, "Well done good and faithful servant" (Matt. 25:21a). On this, I rest.

We who lead local churches share a deep concern. According to the CompareCamp Research Team, only 38 percent of Americans attend church regularly, that meaning every Sunday. Sadly, these statistics point to the alarming fact that 62 percent of Americans seldom, if ever, darken church doors. Numerically, this means that 186,000,000—out of 300,000,000 Americans—will engage in alternate activities this coming Sunday while 114,000,000 attend some house of worship.

Planting a church has by necessity made me a bivocational pastor. By day, I am a hospice chaplain, and I give any energy left in the evenings and on weekends to pastoring my four-year-old church! Frankly, when I think about the previously mentioned research, I wonder where the studies were conducted. My personal experience supports a much lower percentage of regular churchgoers. I think about my last fifty patients, and I'm sad to report that only twelve of them had any kind of faith background. That's only 24 percent!

Contrary to what many think, my association with builders (born between 1927 and 1945) and boomers (1946 to 1964) indicates they have largely forsaken any kind of faith tradition. Generally speaking, I surmise that the Great Depression (1929–1933), World War II (1941–1945), the Korean Conflict (1950–1953), the Vietnam War (1961–1975), the drug culture, the dissolution of moral absolutes, and more took a toll on religious thought and practice in this country. Of course, based on the many heart-rending stories I hear, other factors play into this low percentage as well. These behind-the-scenes stories reveal much mental and emotional pain. Accelerated alcohol and drug-related deaths make me weep. Pollsters provide numbers; individuals tell the heartbreaking stories behind the statistics. As a church leader, I wonder why attendance declined when historically people were in desperate straits. Why did so many back door exits occur during these decades?

My intention with this research and personal encounters is not to bring shame or condemnation, but to sound the alarm. *I believe that strong local churches constitute America's saving grace.* And I don't apologize for making what may seem to many an outlandish statement. I dogmatically believe that any community's greatest asset is its Christ-honoring churches. We've heard it said for years that "it takes a village to raise a child." I'm going to take this truth to a higher level and say, "It takes strong, life-giving churches to redemptively and positively impact culture." Again, the purpose for this writing is to ask the hard questions and to explore the reasons why so many leave local churches. And at the same time provide solutions!

Questions to Ponder

1. How has your local church changed since COVID-19?

2. Be honest. Were you a regular attender before COVID-19?

3. Many local churches have gone virtual (online) during COVID-19. What are the pros and cons of this move?

4. What do you miss about your pre-COVID-19 church?

5

All in the Family

$\mathcal{I}$ came to saving faith because of a local church that weekly proclaimed the unsearchable riches of Jesus Christ. Located on the outskirts of my community, this small church reached into my boyhood and introduced me to the redeeming source of life and subsequently, my life's direction. Where would the future have taken me had I not found new life in Christ and allowed saving grace to lead me? The local church fascinated me as a boy and that fascination has multiplied over the years! Sunday services (morning and evening), Sunday school, revival meetings, vacation Bible schools, water baptisms, funerals, weddings, Christmas and Easter celebrations, family get-togethers, musicals, worship, Bible preaching, baby dedications, youth and children programs, and a multitude of other occasions find their expression at church.

Later, I raised my four children to love the local church. My constant prayer for them was that they, too, would spend their lives serving the Lord through the church, the world's primary soul-saving venue. Jesus loved the Church so much and proved his love by dying on the Cross. He died so the big "C" would carry out its mission through the local "c." I will always remember my younger son asking me one day, "Daddy, if you weren't the pastor and we weren't the pastor's kids, would we go to church as much as we do?" I quickly and proudly responded, "Yes, we would!" As already stated, the local church constitutes a family. Just as the family is the cornerstone of society, the church family is the cornerstone for God's wonderful people.

Let me tell you why the enemy attacks families like he does. He knows that strong families build strong churches and vice versa! If the enemy can tear the spiritual fabric of the home, he automatically compromises the local church. Similarly, the coronavirus has been especially hard on individuals who beforehand had compromised immune systems. Many have died from the virus because they had previously combined life-threatening comorbidities. In the same manner, the enemy effectively weakens the local church by attacking already spiritually compromised homes.

I've often heard it said, "The devil is stupid." However, I'm not sure where that leaves us! The Scriptures remind us that the enemy is a master strategist, and that "we dare not be ignorant of his devices" (2 Cor. 2:11). In short, the enemy has weakened the local church by weakening the home. Please stop and pray right now for your home, your children, grandchildren, and other family members. Just as our family of origin shapes our values and morals, nurtures us, and provides sustenance, the local church affords similar benefits and much more! Heaven will be largely populated by those who began their spiritual journey in a Christ-preaching church.

Paul emphatically states that he (God) "chose the foolishness of preaching to save those who believe" (1 Cor. 1:21). Sadly, many in today's Christian subculture belittle and even deny the need for local churches, and they particularly bemoan the idea of visible church buildings housing the "invisible Church." They dislike hearing, "The Church goes to church." Local churches win the lost to Christ, disciple believers, provide a platform to support world missions, nurture children and youth, thus guaranteeing generational perpetuity, and so much more.

The local church is a family, and families don't give up on one another. Individuals who do not view their church as a "family of believers" will most likely not invest their time, talents, finances, and lives there. It will be simply a place to go on Sunday if or when the mood strikes, and a place to draw on only as needed. Some dismiss church if they get a perceived better offer. This, however, is "going" to church, without "being" the church. Those who simply attend a local church, but do not see themselves as "the church" will likely have no staying power.

Questions to Ponder

1. What were several positive attributes about your family of origin? Negative?

2. What role has the local church played in your life?

3. Do you think most people who attend church see their church as a family? Why or why not?

4. What can you do personally to create a family atmosphere in your church?

6

The Church Goes to Church

$\mathcal{T}$he Scriptures make it clear that God's people have always and will always acknowledge "places of meeting." Let's begin by reading Exodus 25:8, "Then have them make a sanctuary for me, that I may dwell with them." This tent of meeting—Tabernacle in the wilderness—housed God's tangible presence during Israel's wilderness wanderings. God dwelled in a tent made by hands! How exciting and perhaps tiring it was when the cloud located directly above the Tabernacle would lift and move. Israel knew to pack up and follow Yahweh's wilderness itinerary. And how intriguing that nightfall was lit by the fire of God's presence as it rose above the Ark. All eyes focused on this wonderful spectacle of God's glory! Israel understood the wonder of "a place."

Psalm 122:1 supports the same concept of a place designated by God: "I was glad when they said unto me, 'Let us go into the house of the Lord.'" This, of course, refers to Solomon's Temple. This wonder of the ancient world was recognized as a place by Jews and Gentiles alike, where Israel's God showcased his presence among his chosen people. Scholars believe the destruction of Solomon's Temple in Jerusalem in 587 BC gave rise to synagogues, which were subsequently used for public worship and private instruction. Synagogues became each community's gathering place. Jesus taught in the local synagogues of his day. Again, God led the people to gather under one roof. Old Testament patterns and instructions led the Israelites to look toward gathering places, where the people would congregate to hear God's law. Often, they met in the Temple Court, or in open squares.

One of my favorite accounts is found in Nehemiah 8 when Ezra the priest read the Law to the people who stood in the street, as it were.

> And all the people gathered themselves together as one man into the street...and they spoke unto Ezra the scribe to bring the Book of the Law of Moses, which the Lord had commanded to Israel. And Ezra the priest brought the Law before the congregation both of men and women, and all that could hear with understanding, upon the first day of the seventh month. And he read therein before the street...from the morning until midday...and the ears of the people were attentive unto the Book of the Law. And Ezra opened the Book in the sight of all the people, and when he opened it, all the people stood up. And Ezra blessed the Lord, the great God. And all the people answered, "Amen, Amen", with lifting up their hands; and they bowed their heads, and worshipped the Lord with their faces to the ground. (8:1–3, 5–6)

It is obvious that community was necessary and commanded in order for the Israelites to receive instruction and maintain their ongoing identity as God's people. Theirs was often an outdoor meeting place.

Now, let's look at New Testament patterns regarding the importance of Christian community. Most theologians acknowledge the Christian Church was birthed on the Day of Pentecost in AD 29, as recorded in Acts 2. One hundred twenty men and women received the promised Holy Spirit outpouring in an upper room somewhere in Jerusalem. Afterward, following their Savior's command, the disciples of Jesus spread out across the Roman Empire, teaching, preaching the good news of salvation, and healing the sick (Matt. 4:23). And everywhere they went, churches were planted. New converts gathered with those of like, precious faith in recognized communities. Saul turned Paul after his conversion, and later wrote two-thirds of the New Testament. Many of his letters were written to address specific issues in given churches. Paul, for example, wrote an eclectic letter "to the church of God which is at Corinth" (1 Cor. 1:2). His letter to the Galatians was a circular letter written "to the churches of Galatia" (Gal. 1:2). And so on.

Organized groups of believers—the ecclesia, or "called out ones"—gathered in cities everywhere. It appears the Church in Jerusalem became the "Mother Church" for the first-century move of God. It was from Jerusalem the great missionary-evangelistic enterprise spread, and churches quickly sprang up across regions beyond. The same principle and practice holds true today. For instance, when my wife and other team members go to Kenya to preach to the Maasai tribe, they often see entire villages come to faith in Christ. Afterward, new believers meet under trees until buildings can be constructed. Crude structures are built to house these precious converts. Local churches spot the landscapes of Kenya where community is fostered and "a new place" becomes home! These structures also afford congregations protection from vicious predators!

Admittedly, first-century churches met primarily in homes. The New Testament supports the fact that Christians continued to gather in recognized groups and areas long after the day of Pentecost. As a matter of fact, the book of Hebrews was written approximately forty years after the birth of the Church, and the writer emphatically states in 10:24–25,

> "And let us consider how to stimulate one another to love and good deeds, not forsaking our own assembling together, as is the habit of some, but encouraging one another, and *all the more* as you see the day drawing near."

The writer seems to indicate the end time Church will see many Christians forsaking local churches. He counters this unfortunate, even frightening prospect with an admonition to gather all the more.

Now fast-forward 250 years. Roman Emperor Constantine converted to Christianity in 312 AD, and then encouraged the building of buildings! Up to this time, most Christian endeavors originated from private homes. Proponents of the home church movement are exactly right when they say the Early Church primarily met in homes during its first three centuries. However, larger groups of Christians met in warehouses, dining halls, atriums, and other venues. For the purpose of this book, I choose not to emphasize where Christians meet for worship, but rather the ongoing activity of the Holy Spirit in their midst. The bottom line is they have to meet somewhere! Preaching, teaching, praying, and fellowship by virtue of their context happen where people gather.

Perhaps we have over-emphasized architecture versus individual believers being God's "workmanship" (Eph. 2:10). Surely, the Lord is building His "temples"! We are first and foremost commanded to build the kingdom of God, not major on the construction of church buildings. Let me lay this to rest for those who argue that the church is not a building; it is people. I agree! When we make a building more important than kingdom advancement, we skew God's original design.

However, I live in snow country, and I'm so thankful for church structures in northeastern Ohio. Winter weather could prove to be problematic for those who gather, if they had to meet outside! That's why we say, "The Church goes to church." Big "C" finds expression and a place to gather in the little "Cs!" Somewhere along the way, however, church buildings began to spring up everywhere. The Roman Catholic Church is responsible for building some of earth's grandest edifices. Many are simply breathtaking. That's why when Paris's Notre-Dame Cathedral burned on April 15, 2019, people around the world openly wept. For many centuries this magnificent cathedral served as a gathering place for faithful Catholics.

The Reformers would centuries later build their own versions of church structures. Then, with these structures came church governance and of necessity, internal rules and regulations that would govern the use of individual buildings. I'll be honest, whatever man puts his hands to usually becomes characterized by unreasonable control and less than perfect infrastructures. And over time, I suppose that many in all denominations have elevated church buildings above God's original purpose to win the lost and disciple new converts. Today, when people talk about church, it's usually about a specific building at the corner of such and such streets, instead of referring to blood-bought, redeemed people.

Rather than defend church buildings, let me say that the church is made up of people who have been saved by the blood of Jesus and who have placed their trust and faith in his atoning work on the Cross. But it stands to reason the work of God is best carried out in recognized "places of meeting," where Christians gather for community, worship, teaching, preaching, and perpetuity. Just think. How would we finance and organize world missions endeavors except through local churches? How would the lost come to faith were it not for Christ-preaching local churches that present the Gospel, and offer individuals a time and place to respond?

I care not whether it's in someone's home or in a locally recognized house of worship; in an abandoned warehouse, at the Crystal Cathedral in Garden Grove, California; the Compaq Center in Houston, Texas; or under a tree in Kenya. The point is, God's people need a recognized meeting place. Neither is the purpose of this book to discuss the many types of churches or theological persuasions. Entire books have been written about these subjects! The concern of this author is that believers in Christ are either jumping from church to church or simply leaving churches en masse. This writing addresses the reasons why, in an attempt to throw open our front doors and close our back doors!

Again, I wish to ask the hard questions that expose counterproductive reasons behind people leaving local churches, no matter their location, theology, or governance. In the process, I may discover legitimate reasons, and may God give me the boldness and grace to confront any misgivings on my part, or the part of leaders in general, in order to rectify some of this negative movement away from local churches. Under New Testament grace, we who love the Lord are now the "temples of the Holy Spirit" (1 Cor. 6:19–20). He has set up his abode in our lives. We, who have placed our faith in the atoning work of Jesus Christ for the forgiveness of our sins, now recognize that we need community. We need the family of God around us. We dare not live in isolation from the very source that has introduced us to this new life! All excuse making must stop. Our identity as the blood bought finds its greatest joy and expression while gathering together.

Questions to Ponder

1. How does Exodus 25:8 foreshadow today's church?

2. When was the modern church movement birthed?

3. What warning does Hebrews 10:25–26 sound for the local church?

4. Why, in your opinion, is faithful attendance to a local church so important?

5. Why do Christians need community?

7

More Miss Than Hit

*W*hy do so many in the American Church randomly come and go? Why do they attend services in a hit-and-miss fashion? And why do they leave without saying goodbye? What is the attraction away from God's house? I recently read, "Those who often miss church eventually don't miss church!" The enemy of our soul not only desensitizes hearts but pulls affection for Christian community away to lesser pursuits. Sleeping in a garage all night does not make us cars, and going to church every time the doors are open does not automatically make us Christians! We get that, don't we? However, I believe there's a definite correlation between dedicated Christians and church attendance.

We attend church because we love the Lord—period. In Revelation 2:1–4, Jesus issues the following indictment against the Church at Ephesus:

> I know your deeds and your toil and perseverance, and that you cannot tolerate evil men, you put to the test those who call themselves apostles, and they are not, and you found them to be false; and you have perseverance and have endured for My name's sake, and have not grown weary. But I have this against you, that you have left your first love.

Did you know that the greatest enemy of the Christ-follower may very well be mediocrity? Ask the Lord to rekindle your first love!

We must always relish the beauty and the wonder of our salvation. The greatest event of our life is the day—the moment—we accepted Jesus Christ as Savior and Lord. Never get over your salvation! Never be ashamed when the Holy Spirit washes over you during worship. Tears flow when our God-designed tear ducts release liquid prayers! Never undervalue the miracle of forgiveness. In a cemetery not far from New York City is a headstone engraved with a single word: *forgiven.* The message is simple and unembellished. There is no date of birth, no epitaph. There is only a name and the solitary word, *forgiven.* But it is the greatest word that can be applied to any man or woman, or written on any gravestone. It is earth's most precious word! Why not praise him for your salvation this very moment?

I'm afraid that decisions to forsake local churches could result in the loss of first love experiences that keep us tender toward the Lord. Continued absenteeism from God's house could even result in eternal loss. God forbid! With this being said, an obvious correlation continues to exist between low church attendance and spiritual decline.

People fascinate me. They represent both the church's greatest asset and its grandest challenge. Pastors have jokingly said for years, "Ministry would be great if it wasn't for people!" But it is for people, and it's now time to take a deeper look at why so many exit our doors, never to return. And most of them leave quietly without saying goodbye.

If you attend a party or any function for that matter, and you make your exit without saying goodbye, you create suspicion around your leaving. The French refer to this as "ghosting." Social protocol refers to the "art of absquatulating." Does leaving a church without saying goodbye make you an "absquatulator" (my word)? Maybe! "Was he mad?" some ask. Others wonder, "Did something happen to precipitate his abrupt departure?" "How rude," most would think. "He left without saying goodbye." You see, leaving should happen with a period, not a question mark! A sense of uneasiness always pervades questionable departures.

As stated previously, the local church is a family. The very same issues that arise in blood families, also arise in church families. The comparisons are many and important to understand. I get it. Hope Community is not for everyone, and neither is your church, but when family members make abrupt exits, the rest of the family is left to wonder. Everyone is taken by surprise when those we care about leave without saying goodbye. It leaves an empty place at the table, with those still sitting there pondering the "whys." It truly is disconcerting for other family members when loved ones suddenly leave the table to eat elsewhere. These times are both confounding and heart-wrenching.

Someone we love has chosen to leave the family, usually for reasons unknown. Questioning minds are left to wonder. I have discovered that most people leave without the courtesy of a goodbye because they avoid potential conflict at every level. This is proof that many who disagree with something or someone, find it difficult to discuss without becoming disagreeable, or without displaying righteous conduct. Or some are just cowards and refuse to leave righteously or fairly. Will we ever get to the point where we can disagree amicably, and without becoming contentious and negative in our approach to people? We can still love people with whom we disagree.

Is there ever a time to leave a church? I suppose so, but leaving should be the exception. We just don't give up on family! That is, unless we're in the wrong family, or we were never part of the family to begin with. I've seen folks come into the church who simply did not fit. The church's vision, theology, worship expressions, and overall personality did not suit them. In short, they were uncomfortable. This is perfectly fine, and these persons do well to keep searching for the right fit.

Remember, however, there are no perfect churches and none that can meet all the items on unreasonably long "shopping lists." Consumerism must not reign when it comes to church "shopping." I believe we are called to specific faith communities, where our individual gifts can find expression and bring unity and blessing to the entire church family. People need to find a place where they belong and stay put! I've said for years, "One of the greatest miracles on earth is a growing, healthy church." When we consider the diverse personalities, families of origin, hurts, habits, and hang-ups, incorrect teaching, individual idiosyncrasies, socioeconomic backgrounds, and other factors, a solid local church clearly proves that the Gospel brings unity in diversity.

So why do people leave without saying goodbye? I would like to submit the following forty observations. Please understand. This is not an exhaustive list. Your experience may include other reasons. Because most people leave unexpectedly, suddenly, and without the courtesy of an explanation, these observations are speculative only. I suppose entire books could be written on each topic, so of necessity, I only scratch the surface with each discussion. If you currently pastor a church, or have in the past, see if you can relate to any of the following teachings and observations. Let's begin (in no specific order of significance).

Questions to Ponder

1. Before you read the following chapters, why, in your opinion, do people leave local churches?

2. "Those who often miss church eventually do not miss church." What do you think happens?

3. When individuals leave local churches for reasons unknown, how does this affect the entire church?

Part 2

In chapters 7–45, I discuss forty direct and indirect reasons why people and pastors leave churches. The reasons usually mesh. My insights come after much introspection and personal experience. After identifying the issue, I submit solutions while providing teaching moments.

After completing my undergraduate studies in 1978, I was ordained and went on to pastor six churches. Had I known then what lay ahead, I believe I might have jumped that ship for an easier cruise! But since none of us can redo our life's story, we are called to use both our successes and failures to help others. Experience, then, becomes our teacher and our legacy.

At any rate, I was ready to make a difference in my world and was mostly convinced that Paul was not the author of Hebrews! Then reality hit. After people began leaving my churches, I learned that while college had prepared me to preach, only the Lord himself could help me navigate the many day-to-day challenges of ministry.

Identifying problem areas without providing potential solutions is an exercise in futility and total frustration. Principle without application is pointless. As previously stated, I don't have all the answers, but the following chapters touch on areas of concern that at some point attempt to infiltrate all churches.

8

Doubting the Goodness of God

$\mathcal{J}$t is not uncommon for me to meet people who are mad at God. When they hear that I'm a chaplain-pastor, it's "talk to the hand" time. They shut me down, convinced that God is the reason behind their present predicament. I hear one of two arguments: (1) "If God loves me, why am I in the mess I'm in?" (2) "If God cares so much, why did He allow this to happen to me?" The first argument accepts no blame for poor decisions. The second argument challenges even the theologians. And both make "me" the center of the universe!

Hurricane Laura ripped through Louisiana in August 2020, leaving behind a path of death and destruction. At the same time, fires swept through Northern California, scorching over four million acres, according to the California Department of Forestry and Fire Protection, and by summer's end, thirty-one people lost their lives. We would do well to place the blame for natural disasters where it rightfully belongs. The Bible teaches that he (Satan) is "the ruler of the kingdom of the air" (Eph. 2:2b). Insurance companies need to reconsider their thinking as well. Natural disasters are inappropriately described as "acts of God." Tragedy abounds all around us. Is God to blame?

Some, even ministers of the Gospel, teach that God uses natural disasters and tragedy in general to judge us. A nurse friend of mine was told after her newborn died that it was God's judgment on her for becoming pregnant out of wedlock. That pastor did not help the cause of those who believe that God is good rather than punitive in His approach to people. And guess what? That woman has not attended church since that fateful conversation twenty-eight years ago. And by the way, she was also told that the baby went to hell because she and her boyfriend at the time were not believers. How sad!

I believe that God is good. The Bible clearly reveals his loving nature. "For God is love" (1 John 4:8b). And He "demonstrated his love toward us in that while we were yet sinners, Christ died for us" (Rom. 5:8). One of my favorite verses and one that I often dissect at funeral services is John 3:16. "For God so loved the world that he gave his only Son that whoever believes in him will not perish, but have eternal life." He didn't just love, he "so loved"! Do you sense the divine intensity in this verse? Not only does God love the world, he so-o-o-o-loves the world! Yes, God's nature, his very essence is love. As a matter of fact, he is the complete expression of love!

So what about the massive destruction we read about in the Old Testament? You know, where God incinerates twin cities? Where God supposedly kills Mr. and Mrs. Job's ten children? Where God allows King David's baby to die? And on and on. And what about Revelation chapters 6–18, which record God's wrath as it is poured out upon the earth? It does seem incongruous that a good God is associated with such doings. However, the Scriptures overall declare the goodness of God. Some of the events recorded in the Bible that people commonly use to justify their claim that God is harsh include events in Genesis—the fall of man, the flood, Sodom and Gomorrah, and then they proceed to the Canaanites, Egyptians, Benjamites, and even move on to non-Christians in general. Obviously, plenty of other examples in Scripture elicit questions.

Consider the analogy of a person who steals and gets caught. When he stands before the judge, the judge finds him guilty and imposes a fine. But then, the judge offers to pay the fine. Instead, the thief refuses and blames the whole mess on the judge who acted justly and even offered a way out. Likewise, God's track record of mercy is impeccable. He offered a way of escape for all of the above incidents in the Old Testament, and for us as well. God, through

Christ, offers mankind a way of escape out of his sinful condition. And what you read in Revelation comes to the earth after God repeatedly tries to win lost mankind after having been rejected. God is holy and his holiness mandates a verdict. This is really what is happening in today's culture. Mankind sins and gets caught. People are found guilty by a holy God. God then steps in and offers a means of salvation from the punishment of the crime (which is eternal death), even so far as to die in their place so they can have eternal life.

Yet in all this, some people refuse to yield their lives to God and then proceed to blame him for the situation they are in. It simply doesn't make sense. In light of this, God should not be blamed, but those who were punished for their sin retain the blame. God did provide a means of salvation in each of the above cases, even though he was not obligated to. God should not be blamed. Interestingly enough, individuals who say God is cruel demand justice when they are wronged. For example, if someone steals from them or attacks them or offends them in any way, they exhibit a double standard. We are all sinners under the death penalty. Both Romans 5:12 and 1 Corinthians 15:21 remind us that "death came by sin." And with sin came sickness and suffering. Sin also brought separation from God. Romans 3:23 makes it clear: "For all have sinned and fall short of the glory of God." But again, God has promised a way of escape, a means of salvation in Christ.

We need to blame the devil who is the real culprit, not our wonderful God who provides a way out! Jesus reminds us, "The thief comes only to steal, kill and destroy, and I came to bring life, and that more abundant" (John 10:10). Those who have left local churches after blaming God for some tragedy in their lives need to reconsider to whom the blame is due. Our loving Lord patiently awaits their return to the God of the house and the house of God!

Questions to Ponder

1. Have I blamed God for any tragedy in my life?

2. If I have shifted blame toward God and left the church, in what local church do I need to make a new start?

3. Have you memorized John 3:16? Do it today!

4. The term "acts of God" blames God for natural calamities. What is your thinking regarding the origin of hurricanes, tornadoes, earthquakes, typhoons, and other natural phenomena?

9

Virtual Church

Thank God for the internet, the worldwide web. It has opened up an inexhaustible source of information for all to benefit. You name it. What we need comes at the touch of our fingertips! Google is our friend! The prophet Daniel told us the end times would be marked by an increase of knowledge (12:4), and here we are! However, as I look around, I see signs that the internet has also brought ongoing negative changes to our former way of life.

Before I continue, please understand my observations are age-driven and not necessarily the opinion of all post-baby boomers! Newspapers have all but disappeared. Many Christian bookstores have closed their doors. Businesses that we once took for granted are gone because the internet has made their commodities available on innumerable shopping websites. Amazon has proven to be a source of convenience and necessity for many during the coronavirus pandemic! Malls across the nation have either closed, or their parking lots remain mostly empty. Again, Google has made possible an information explosion. Recent reports indicate that 35 percent of all internet downloads are related to pornography. Because most anyone has access to computer website construction, many sites cannot be trusted in terms of informational accuracy. This is problematic. Download with caution!

And here's the kicker in terms of the local church, COVID-19, and the internet: A large number of Christians traded church attendance for online services. And of course, many pastors felt it right to use online ministry to protect their beloved church. This is absolutely commendable. And wise! The tension between obeying those in government authority versus prudent Christian service has prompted leaders to ask, "What's the right thing to do at any given time?" I personally know a very heartbroken pastor who moved to online services when the COVID-19 pandemic hit the United States. When things opened back up after the first wave, his church did not return! They scattered and never came back. Today the church building is for sale. I've heard a lot of sad stories during my lifetime, but this one nearly tops the list. My pastor friend still openly weeps over his situation.

I appreciate television ministries, internet online services and Facebook Time for those unable to worship in a local church. These venues provide wonderful opportunities for the less fortunate to indirectly connect with services around the country and world. Thank God for online ministries that provide spiritual food for the infirmed, shut-ins, and others who can no longer attend church services.

On the flipside, we still need to encourage local church attendance. It's one thing to hear a service on the internet, but greater still is the beauty and power of one-on-one fellowship and Christian community. Online pastors, radio or television ministries do not make house calls. Neither do they make hospital calls or provide one-on-one counseling opportunities. They cannot lay their hands on the sick. Nor can they hug necks or offer comfort and help during life's good and bad times. The spiritual intensity of local church gatherings far outweighs the more indirect appeal of internet church.

Sitting on the couch watching an internet service pales in comparison to the wonder of local gatherings where the anointing of the Holy Spirit and the wonder of spiritual connection impacts precious lives who come together in unity with the Lord, oneness in the Spirit, and love for one another. Statistics regarding the internet and its impact on local church attendance have yet to be released; however, when it's all said and done, the online church will surely be a factor in the local church's numerical decline. We, who love the interaction of coming together, while thankful for online alternatives, must never allow them to permanently replace our physical presence in a house of worship.

Questions to Ponder

1. What are some positive aspects of the internet as they pertain to the local church?

2. What are some negative aspects of the internet as they pertain to the local church?

3. Is there ever a time to replace church attendance with online services?

10

All Aboard?

As you know, churches embrace all kinds of governing patterns. My observation and overall concern is that "too many chiefs and very few Indians" make for inevitable strife and division. Many have disassociated themselves from the stress that accompanies church dissension. Control freaks vie for titles and positions. Jesus most definitely displayed servanthood over positional leadership. The king of glory washed his disciples' feet and by this act of humility demonstrated that serving others was our primary responsibility in the kingdom of God. It's not about us; it's about serving others. When we serve others, we serve God!

How many people come into churches with unreasonable expectations? "How can this church serve me?" Or "What can I expect from this church?" This is the antithesis of what Jesus taught. Still, others come into local churches to promote their own agenda. They lack humility. In my opinion, positional mind-sets have no place in local churches.

Many wonderful people have been wounded in the crossfires of provocation and power plays. It appears the American Church has largely embraced democratic mind-sets as their governing pattern. Please remember, however, while we may live in a democracy (really a republic), where voting, individual opinions and the right of expression are king, the local church is best served by theocratic mind-sets. In other words, God chooses one man or in many cases one woman, to move individual faith communities forward. Of course, righteous accountability from wise counselors is always necessary.

With this being said, churches that utilize boards must first be reminded that boards are primarily used by corporate America for legal and fiducial purposes. Everyone has an opinion that often becomes counterproductive to the overall health of the organization. Power plays and tension are often the result. Board supervised churches often negate the biblical role of pastor, reducing him or her to a hireling status (see chapter 11). Many on church boards may challenge this statement; however, the fact remains that board-run churches only move forward when pastors are given their rightful authority. I suppose that boards who view their role in strictly an advisory capacity have a greater chance of realizing a pleasant pastor-board relationship. However, this governing model more often than not exalts the desires and opinions of men and challenges the God-given authority of theocratic rule.

I heard a pastor say, "Had Moses gathered a committee around himself, the Israelites would still be in Egypt!" And I agree. Majority rule may work for corporate America, but God never placed much confidence in its outcome. Consider the story of the spies in Numbers 13. Moses sent out twelve men to scout out the Promised Land. Ten of the spies returned, shaken to their core, saying in essence, "Did you see the size of those giants?" Only two of the spies—Joshua and Caleb—came back with a faith-filled report. They countered the ten men by asking, "Yes, we saw the giants, but did you see the size of those grapes?" They chose to emphasize God's greatness instead of the giants' size. Had majority rule been utilized, Israel would have been victimized by ten men instead of moving forward at the report of two men who faced reality head-on yet understood that their faith in God would make a way for them. To be sure, they saw the giants (obstacles) but were more impressed by the grapes (God's promises). The New York Giants may have won the pennant in 1951, but thankfully, another kind of giant lost in approximately 1428 BC!

Many denominations in the United States embrace the board model of government. Everything within me, however, challenges this misguided model. I have pastored five churches that had a

59

strong board presence. So based on personal experience, I feel strongly we must flee from any model that exalts voting, majority rule, and democratic mind-sets over pastoral authority. God's design has always been—Old and New Testament—one man or woman receiving their marching orders from the throne and communicating vision to the people. Accountability is essential, but controlling attitudes often hold back local churches from realizing their God-given potential. To place the local church in the hands of a board is to nullify God's original design. Whoever said that all the men or women on any given board are always hearing from God and care about the church in the same way as the pastor? And where in the Scriptures do we find where God's people were led effectively by more than one recognized leader? The answer is nowhere! To be sure, wise leaders empower and train others to come alongside them in the work of the local church. But there can only be one head! The apostle Paul wrote to Titus, "For this reason, I left you in Crete, that you would set in order what remains and appoint elders in every city as I directed you" (1:5). To be sure, the pastor was the recognized leader in each church.

In the book of Acts, the history book of the Early Church, we find local churches being led by bishops, elders, or pastors, which are all basically synonymous terms. Deacons were chosen in Acts 6 to come alongside the local elder so that he might "not neglect the ministry of the Word" (verse 4). For American churches to elect boards and operate according to *Robert's Rules of Order* is an invitation to disaster. To liken Acts 6:1–4 to boards is to superimpose a twenty-first-century fiducial practice on a first-century servant leadership mind-set. Churches under this type of government model usually struggle to move forward because strong personalities rule and weaker personalities have to be subdued. Pastors often are called to mediate potential disagreements. And most always, they end up on the losing side of an impending emotionally-filled rift.

It was this type of church government that nearly ruined me—mentally, emotionally, and spiritually. I strongly urge churches everywhere who embrace this model to reconsider their approach. I realize, however, that local churches under the umbrella of denominations that embrace board governance have no alternative. Their only recourse is to abide by denominational protocol.

Over the years, a good number of people have left these churches and attempted to find a place in nondenominational, elder-run churches, only to still struggle. When are we going to put aside man-made governance and do it God's way? At Hope Community, we emphasize servant leadership and eldership advisory. Accountability measures are put in place, and gifted, willing people are given freedom to enjoy their leadership responsibilities. Those who are used to a democratic leadership model are often victimized by said model and find it difficult to stay in churches where they have little or no say in terms of church direction. It's a hard juxtaposition for some to overcome. Democratic mind-sets, although often disdained by many, are hard to break.

Look at the following direct quotes followed by my responses from exit interviews of people who left my congregations and note the pronoun use in each one.

"The worship leader refused to lead songs that I recommended." *It's not about your likes or dislikes. It's about everyone entering into God's presence, regardless of the song choices. Let the worship leader lead!*

"Your sermons were irrelevant." *It could be that you need to open your spirit to receive the pastor's words.*

"I missed three Sundays in a row and nobody, including you (the pastor), called me." *Do you call individuals who miss services? My guess is no!*

"You need to move the service time as I need my sleep." *It's not about your convenience.*

"*I* told you to go visit my sister and you never did." *"I told…"* *How sad. I can't imagine telling a pastor to do anything or treating him or her like this. He's not your hired hand; He's God's gift to your church, and he's doing everything he can to help you get to heaven! You don't tell him; you kindly ask him.*

It is my strong opinion that many churches are seeing declining attendances because of democratic mind-sets that produce "churchy" attitudes, extol individual rights, and minimize true Christian love.

It often seems that people are more concerned about church policy and protocol than winning souls.

Sadly, large numbers of churches have turned membership into a country club mentality. They pay dues that they feel entitles them to certain benefits. Entitlement mentalities have replaced servant mentalities, thus creating a self-serving attitude in many churches. I have noticed that a lot of believers are keen about discussing their church, but squeamish when talking about their Jesus. It galls me when believers get together and dissect their church, pastor, programs, opinions, and discuss other people in the church often in a negative light, and never one time talk about the goodness of the Lord, Scripture, or Christian virtues. I have always believed that most fall-out in local churches results over "churchiness," not Jesus. Eyes and hearts kept on Jesus always deemphasize church buildings, pastoral performance, programs, and infrastructures. They remember that Jesus died for the Church, not a building or to hold a secure position. And their heart's desire is to serve, not to be served.

I searched my heart before and after writing about church governance. Some may accuse me of being angry. This may have been the case some years ago; however, what I write today comes from a broken heart, as I again review the devastation I've personally experienced and similar stories from many pastor friends regarding their board-run churches. Would employees dare go to work and tell their boss, "This is how things are going to be run from now on?" Of course not! So what makes Christians think they have the right to order their pastor around, scrutinize him unfairly, or minimize his God-given authority? Churches that mistreat their pastor or do not recognize his righteous calling will continue to see decline. God smiles on churches that bless their pastor and support him with their prayers, loyalty, and attendance.

Questions to Ponder

1. What gifts/strengths do I have to help my church move forward?

2. What can I do to encourage my pastor?

3. Do I need to repent of any misguided attitudes toward my church or pastor?

4. Does my church honor our pastor on special occasions—birthdays, anniversaries, Christmas, during Pastor Appreciation Month (October)?

5. Does our church respect our pastor's day off?

11

Pastor or Hireling?

As previously suggested, churches that impact their communities are led by one recognized leader. Vision for the church and community flows through the pastor. And everything that occurs must filter through the pastor's vision. Otherwise, churches struggle with "division." All who serve as leaders in a given body must joyfully and loyally follow the leadership of the pastor who carries the right to make changes and alterations as he deems necessary for the forward movement of the church. Every ministry in the local church must be seen as "part of the whole." One must never function as its own entity. Just as malignant cells in the human body rebel against healthy cells and cause disease, individuals who rebel against pastoral vision become "tumors" in the local body.

During my first pastorate, a boy's ministry began to operate totally separate from the body life of the church. As a matter of fact, the leader pulled the boys aside during service times and held separate meetings. He undermined my authority as pastor by modeling disloyalty and a subversive attitude. I had to dismiss the man because of his rebellious attitude. He possessed an Absalom spirit, which had to be confronted (read 2 Samuel 15:1–12). Pastors surely must walk in the wisdom of the Lord! Everything in the local church must flow through the pulpit. What does this mean? The preached Word of God is any church's greatest asset. Nothing takes precedence over the preached Word. And I mean nothing!

Individual ministries or programs in the local church must come into line with the pulpit message and the pastor's heart. Usurping the pastor's authority creates church dissension. Those who refuse to come under the pastor's vision usually display a contentious heart. Because many churches see their pastor as a "hired hand," such comments seem incongruous and almost smack of arrogance. However, in my opinion, both time and results have proven that America needs to get back to a healthier pastor-church leadership model. I firmly believe in apostolic succession, the Bible way. Apostolic succession is usually associated with the Catholic Church; however, in the epistles, it was the recognized method of identifying and placing future leaders from within. "For this reason, I left you in Crete, that you would set in order what remains and appoint elders in every city as I directed you" (Titus 1:5). Future leaders were determined by their faithfulness to the local church, by their consistent godly character and their proven calling and ministry. In my opinion, successful churches today are those that win the lost and then mentor and train from within, subsequently giving the Holy Spirit opportunities to download the spiritual DNA of that house in their spirit.

In the book of Acts and throughout the epistles, we note that Peter and Paul, in particular, placed pastors in local churches, and strong evidence indicates they were lifetime appointments. To promote continuity and to perpetuate ministry, churches raised up their own future leaders who grew up learning the church's specific vision (assignment). This practice promoted stability and pastors-elders-bishops (all the same) were definitely the recognized leader of each church. They "parented" and raised their churches to not only discover new life in Christ but to help their family grow toward maturity.

As a matter of fact, when addressing the Church at Thessalonica, Paul likened himself to both a mother and a father figure among them. "But we proved to be gentle among you, as a nursing *mother* tenderly cares for her own children, having so fond an affection for you, we were well-pleased to impart to you not only the gospel of

God but also our own lives, because you had become very dear to us" (1 Thess. 2:7–8). In verses 10–12, he says,

> You are witnesses, and so is God, how devoutly and uprightly and blamelessly we behaved toward you believers; just as you know how we were exhorting and encouraging and imploring each one of you as a *father* would his own children, so that you would walk in a manner worthy of the God who calls you into his own kingdom and glory.

You can understand why many churches struggle over time, given the many personality types, ministry outlooks, strengths, and weaknesses that rapidly succeeding pastors bring to the helm. I'm afraid we have been encouraged to climb the ranks while using churches as stepping stones to find the bigger, better ministry opportunities. This, too, has created a sense of discontentment among many aspiring young pastors. If I am guilty of anything in ministry, it has been my propensity to become discontented with my present opportunities and challenges. The grass on the other side of the fence always appeared greener! It took me more years than I'm willing to admit to "learn how to be content in whatever circumstance I found myself" (Phil. 4:11).

Yes, there is a time to move on; however, we pastors may need to get before the Lord and seek renewed passion and holy stamina to complete our assignment in a given location. Truthfully, about the time some pastors learn their church, specific community dynamics, and become "mother and father," they leave! May the Lord give pastors bulldog tenacity to push through difficult times and humility to enjoy the good times. Can we again see local churches as families who stick together?

From my standpoint, when churches experience pastoral turnover in rapid succession, it sends entire congregations into a tailspin. Each new pastor, of course, brings his own gifts and vision to the table and understandably, individuals in each church do their best to hold on to already established comfort zones. This reality, I'm afraid, describes where most churches' function—always tenaciously holding on to their past and resisting anything new. I, for example, pastored churches where I followed—with one exception—multiple short-term predecessors, and depending on public sentiment at the time, either lived in the shadow of success or failure. To be honest, I left each church feeling like my tenure was cut short and my ability to succeed placed in jeopardy. In essence, the dynamics under which I pastored made me a stepparent. I was one in a line of stepdads or even big brothers. And we all know the potential for conflict and misplaced influence increases with each new stepparent.

Here's what happens: When pastors are hirelings, they are forced to lead "from the bottom up, instead of the top-down." The "kids" or those in the local church are given misdirected authority. They carry more influence than their parents (pastor). In this system, roles are reversed and the pastor does what the "kids" tell him to do. This role-reversal spells disaster for local churches and highlights committees—based not on apostolic succession, but the whims and preferences of majority rule. The only eventual outcome is tension and conflict. The "kids" lead while the parents (pastors) die a slow death. The average length of stay for pastors in America is four years. Burnout is common and a very sad reality. High pastoral turnover creates a yo-yo effect, whereby one pastor realizes a degree of success (however that is defined); while the next pastor may experience unsympathetic, judgmental attitudes that bring decline. Without some degree of apostolic succession, churches will always build on leadership styles that are less than effective.

In my case, those around me maintained authority while I held responsibility for church growth and development. The workload and success of every service and event was mostly placed on my shoulders. Carrying the responsibility for the church's success without having the necessary authority to make that happen describes the overall fallacy of the church-board model of governance (chapter 10). Sadly, the sin of most pastor-board relationships is the sin of neglect. Board members can, at times, be some of the most unfaithful people in the church. And in my experience, a good number of board members consistently failed to support church activities and meetings with their attendance. Usually, I was powerless to address such leadership malfeasance. It is difficult, if not impossible, to delegate responsibility to positional leaders who desire titles but refuse to invest themselves in the body life of the church. Again, pastoral burnout becomes inevitable.

This system sets pastors up to fail. It does not seem to be working, so why not do it the Bible way? This is not promoting a one-man show, but rather, placing God's original design back into local churches, so they have a chance to move forward. Servant leadership, where service is elevated above titles, where gifts and callings are humbly acknowledged, where everyone has opportunity to help move the local church forward and no one is concerned about who gets the credit, is God's design for the local church. In my mind, servant leadership is nonnegotiable.

Every local church has the same primary assignment—to win the lost to Christ. With this said, some local churches have not seen individuals come to faith in a long time. This should concern every pastor and church. Pastor, if this describes your church, ask the Lord what you can do to stem the tide of barren altars. There are numerous ways to encourage individuals to respond to appeals for salvation. The Lord will lead you in this all-important matter. I've always correlated preaching with fishing, and it seems incongruous to me that any minister would preach and not elicit a response from his listeners. It would be like having a fish on your hook and then not reeling it in!

God also gives each local church secondary assignments. These differ according to the personality, need, and makeup of each community. For example, I know of a church that has a "classic car ministry." The church exists in a community where many own vintage vehicles. I pastor in a county that boasts nineteen historic covered bridges. We participate in the annual "Covered Bridge Festival." Pastors are strategically called to complete the assignment God has placed upon them.

You see, God works through assignments. Our Lord is the primary example of this truth. In Jesus's High Priestly discourse, he prays,

"I have glorified You on the earth. I have finished the work (assignment) You gave me to do" (John 17:4). Jesus was assignment-driven. The apostle Paul also understood that his life was assignment-driven. In 2 Timothy 4:7, he writes, "I have fought the good fight, I have finished the course (assignment), I have kept the faith." Mature, secure pastors understand that God places gifted individuals in their church to help move it forward. That's why I support a servant leadership type of ministry over positional leadership. Jesus, the Son of God, king of glory, and sovereign God came to serve! Servant leaders are God's gift to the church if they understand the absolute necessity of loyalty and submission to the vision of the house. Churches can have only one head. Otherwise, they operate under a call to fail.

When will churches understand this all-important principle? Until then, people who vie for ministry opportunities and control, and who jockey for positions or titles will continue to leave, many times taking others with them. Sadder still is the many times when church leaders call for the pastor's removal, not realizing that their actions potentially bring setbacks that make any forward movement impossible. How many churches are dying in this country because they refuse to understand the dynamics of healthy pastor-church relationships? Again, my strong opinion is that most pastors are set up for failure. And over this, I weep.

Questions to Ponder

1. Every ministry in the local church is "part of the whole." What does this mean?

2. Nothing in the local church takes precedence over the preached Word. What are your thoughts?

3. Why is the pastor who has no authority but carries total responsibility set up for failure in the local church?

4. Do you understand effective apostolic succession? What are the advantages of this practice? Any drawbacks?

12

No Lead-In Material

$\mathcal{P}$oor social skills can and do factor into people leaving churches. Does this reason surprise you? Read on! This discussion will center around my opinion that a notably high percentage of people in today's America never learned effective people skills. They simply do not know how to interact in an occasion-appropriate manner. Time and again, I have watched as newcomers especially, and even "regulars" stand on the sidelines, waiting for someone to approach them. When approached, they answer with one or two words and then provide no "lead-in material"! They are proverbial lumps of clay with limited understanding of social interaction.

Their body language is often misunderstood. It says, "Leave me alone!" In reality, such individuals may be crying out for attention and affection, but they have built an impenetrable cocoon around themselves, causing others to avoid or ignore them. It's so sad! No eye contact, shyness, and hard, uninviting looks make it difficult for others to approach them. These precious people need to understand the principle of the "invisible imprint," or the vibe they give off upon entering a room. Their faces, posture, and overall body language, mixed with their inability to speak, make them prime candidates to be overlooked.

Of course, this is unfortunate, but in reality, who can blame others for their unwillingness to push past hard to approach body language? One man said to me, "This is just the way I am. People need to accept me and quit trying to change me." While I hear what he was saying, my response is one that equalizes the chances for better communication. Individuals with poor, even crippling people skills can learn to present themselves in a more appealing manner. How they act constitutes a learned response. This condition need not be a life sentence.

The good news is that people can change! Arms crossed, eyes glued to the floor, turned heads, poker faces, no eye contact, hands in the pockets, and other visual mannerisms combine to say, "Leave me alone." And out of courtesy, most people will oblige this clearly visible, unspoken request. Often, individuals with poor people skills leave churches, blaming pastors and people in general for being unfriendly and uncaring. This is most unfortunate because the real problem is the guy in the mirror who needs to redress his invisible imprint with smiles, acceptable body language, and improved verbal skills that lead to better exchange. Standing or sitting around, waiting for others to do all the talking and responding is a type of mental cruelty.

Frankly, no one has time for a "project" (see chapter 17), but most are open to a friendly, warm first impression that eventually breaks down communication barriers and paves the way for potential new friendships. Individuals who leave churches due to their poor people skills need to quit blaming others for their apparent shortcomings and determine to push their way through to better verbal skills. If not, they could very well spend their lives friendless and heart-crushingly lonely.

Another group of people may or may not lack in people skills, but they tend to live in seclusion. They prefer to live out their days in quiet isolation. Isolationists are easy to spot. They come into church, walk through the crowd with their eyes fixed straight ahead, find a seat, and wait quietly for the service to begin. They dutifully shake hands with friendlier faces, but their body language says, "Don't talk to me." They usually don't sing and often refuse to participate in other segments of the service as well. Following the dismissal prayer, isolationists again walk out with their hands to their sides, their eyes fixed straight ahead. Their body language again says, "Don't talk to me," and their quick exit reveals their intention to leave as mysteriously as they came.

Isolationists repeat this same pattern week after week; that is, until they either decide to become part of the church's community life or leave altogether. Usually, they leave unannounced and without the courtesy of a conversation. Pastors and churches know nothing about them, for their privacy is paramount and strongly protected. Isolationists are not exactly rude, but neither can they be labeled as friendly. These individuals find it difficult to embrace any faith community long-term because their silence is both mysterious and their behavior makes it difficult for pastors and others to know how to respond to them. Do we push past their apparent barriers and risk offending them, or do we honor their body language and simply smile? The answers are complicated. In my experience, isolationists stay for perhaps six months to a year and then leave as mysteriously as they came. And upon their departure, we still know little or nothing about them. Isolationists come and go, and churches are left to wonder what could have been different in their approach. No longer do I take personal responsibility for the hard-to-explain actions of isolationists.

Everyone has a responsibility to interact at some level in the community of faith. Those who choose to remain distant and unexplainable rob themselves of a potentially rewarding spiritual and familial church experience. It's one thing to be quiet and shy; it's another thing to never lend our lives to those with whom we come into contact. Isolationists, of course, cause us great concern and always a sense of helplessness.

Questions to Ponder

1. What vibes do I give off upon entering a room?

2. How can I improve my social skills?

3. Do I make good eye contact when I speak to people?

4. Have I ever isolated myself from others at church? Why?

5. How can I personally help individuals who self-isolate?

6. The author writes, "Everyone has a responsibility to inter-act at some level in the community of faith." What do you think?

13

Talking Trash

The apostle Paul reminds the young preacher Timothy that in the last days, perilous times will come upon the earth. He then elaborates, naming specific behavioral issues that will characterize many:

> But realize this, that in the last days difficult times will come. For men will be *lovers of self,* lovers of money, boastful, arrogant, revilers, disobedient to parents, ungrateful, unholy, unloving, irreconcilable, *malicious gossips,* without self-control, brutal, haters of good, treacherous, reckless, conceited, lovers of pleasure rather than lovers of God, holding to a form of godliness, although they have denied its power. Avoid such men as these. (2 Tim. 3:1–5)

I believe what Paul described often correlates with why people leave churches. So let me discuss the issue of disloyalty as it leads to betrayal, and ultimately, why both behaviors lead to people making their exit from churches. Disloyalty and betrayal work hand in hand. One brings about the other. The apostle begins by saying, "Men will be lovers of self" (verse 2). This speaks of disloyalty that ends up in betrayal.

Pastors can usually withstand most assaults stemming from personal character issues, but disloyalty and betrayal always seem to bring the final blow. How gut-wrenching to experience these at the hands of trusted people! Our Savior met with disloyalty and betrayal at the hands of Judas Iscariot. He is the Bible's premiere example—poster child—of both. It goes without saying that Judas often usurped the Lord's actions with contempt. Recall the occasion when several of the disciples were dining at the home of Mary, Martha, and Lazarus, not long after Lazarus had been raised from the dead.

> So they made Him a supper there, and Martha was serving, but Lazarus was one of those reclining at the table with Him. Mary then took a pound of very costly perfume of pure nard, and anointed the feet of Jesus and wiped His feet with her hair, and the house was filled with the fragrance of the perfume. But Judas Iscariot, one of His disciples, who was intending to *betray* Him, said, "Why was this perfume not sold for three hundred denarii and given to poor people?" Now he said this, not because he was concerned about the poor, but because he was a thief, and so he had the money box, he used to pillage what was put into it. (John 12:2–6)

Another Bible example of disloyalty leading to betrayal is, of course, Peter, who would deny the Lord three times in one night and later repent. Peter definitely made a wonderful comeback!

We pastors are in the people business. We understand our role includes shepherding broken people. And broken people are apt to sacrifice loyalty at the altar of self-love, and in the case of Peter, self-preservation. How is loyalty defined? "A strong feeling of support or allegiance." Loyalty is a wonderful attribute shared by true friends. What about betrayal? "The violation of a person's trust and confidence."

God's people must be loyal to one another. And betrayal must not be found among local church families. We must not allow our differences, our offenses, and our personal emotional-mental pain cause us to respond to one another through disloyalty and ultimate betrayal. The acid test of our faith is how we treat one another. A look at each of the above end-time behavioral characteristics reveals that they are interrelated. One precipitates the others. May God help us to love one another with the love of the Lord and prove to an onlooking world that serving Jesus Christ truly makes a righteous difference in our relationships.

I admit it. Over the years, I talked about people in my churches. I gossiped. I sinned against the Lord and them. I justified it by saying, "I'm the pastor." Oh, how I regret those times. I have asked the Lord to forgive me, and I believe that because of the blood of Jesus I am forgiven. However, what you and I need to remember is that the old saying, "Sticks and stones may break my bones, but words can never harm me" is not true. Words are forces and words spoken in an unkind, judgmental manner can take years to heal—if then. Fallout in local churches will be avoided if we "treat others like we wish to be treated" (Matt. 7:12). May God help us pastors model righteous conversation and guard our tongues. "Let the words of (my) mouth and the meditation of (my) heart be acceptable in your sight, Oh Lord, my strength and my Redeemer" (Ps. 19:14).

We must be diligent to speak life-giving words (forces) as we mingle with those we serve. Let's admit it, pastors. There are people we are called to shepherd that we don't like. Others we don't trust. We prefer not to be around them. However, they have been entrusted to our care, and they need to feel loved and valued as well. We are called to love them unconditionally. And we must guard our attitude and words. My wife and I have made a pact to be righteous and good to all who call Hope Community "home." That includes the way we talk about them. Because we are pastors does not give us the right to talk trash. That is what author Asher Intrater in his book, *Covenant Relationships: A Handbook for Integrity and Loyalty* calls spiritual murder.

God's people must be loyal to one another, regardless of personal feelings. No one said we have to like one another, but the Scriptures definitely prohibit gossip. "Let no unwholesome talk come out of your mouth" (Eph. 4:29). James 3 speaks about the power of the tongue.

> So also the tongue is a small part of the body, and yet it boasts of great things. See how great a forest is set aflame by such a small fire. And the tongue is a fire, the very world of iniquity; the tongue is set among our members as that which defiles the entire body, and sets on fire the course of our life… With it we bless the Lord and Father, and with it we curse men, who have been made in the likeness of God; from the same mouth come both blessing and cursing. My brethren, these things ought not to be this way. (verses 5–6, 9–10)

God's people are to speak well of one another. And here's where my wife and I endeavor to walk in due diligence toward our brothers and sisters in Christ. We need to speak well of people when their names are mentioned in pleasant conversation. My mother taught me, "If you can't say something nice about someone, don't say anything at all." This should be the theme of any ministry! How wonderful to sit back and know that we have not talked unkindly about anyone in the church. Then, the enemy has no legal right to accuse us. When names are brought up in conversations, we remain silent or if the occasion calls for it, we affirm or speak well of the person being discussed. "How good and how pleasant it is that brethren dwell together in unity" (Ps. 133:1). Again, no one can rightfully lay any charges against us. When we speak with people—whether we like them or not—we can look them in the eyes when we speak and allow the love of Jesus to direct our remarks.

You may ask, why are you highlighting this aspect of loyalty? Because loyalty tells the world that we are "the real deal," and that we can be trusted. Local churches can chase the enemy out of the building and the faith community at large, demonstrating to all that we are truly God's wonderful people. In my mind, few things hurt a local church more than individuals secretly and/or publicly talking negatively about others in the body. I have learned that if individuals gossip about their mates, their children, or their friends, they will most likely do the same about anyone. This is a sad reality, but true. I'm determined to speak well of those I serve in the local church. They are family, and I love them. I want always to be honest and truthful with them, never allowing myself to gossip or break confidences. Like you, I've experienced the pain of disloyalty and betrayal. How it hurts when individuals talk negatively about my sermons, my leadership skills, my weaknesses, and when they exploit my faults and failures for all to hear. Disloyalty from people I trusted, twisted stories, and being quoted out of context all bring terrible pain.

The enemy works hard to bring distrust in our lives and tempts us to withdraw from the very ones we are called to serve. Disloyalty, whether from the pastor or people in general, destroys and causes setbacks in any local church. Pastor friend, be honest. Be real. Be truthful. Guard your words. Speak well of your congregants—to and about them. Your community will take note! I have perhaps rambled, but my heart toward you is that you honor the dignity and right of others to be loved unconditionally, regardless of what *they* say or how *they* talk. The Lord is pleased when his people love and respect one another in this manner.

Questions to Ponder

1. What is the correlation between disloyalty and betrayal?

2. Read 2 Timothy 3:1–5 again. How do these behaviors tie in with people leaving local churches?

3. What is spiritual murder?

14

Slack, Not Flack

$\mathscr{J}$esus taught that one of the trademarks of the end times will be the acceleration of offenses. "And *many* will be offended" (Matt. 24:10). The outcome of embracing offenses is twofold: People *betray* one another and *hate* one another. The final outcome is people turning away from the Lord: "And *many will turn away* from Me." The devil loves it when God's people become offended. Individuals use offenses as an excuse to belittle what Jesus died for—the Church. Their emotional pain overrides the beauty of the local church and its reason for being.

I admit it. Christians tend to be hard on one another. They often take on a corrective posture when in conversation. They nitpick. They major in the minors. Nobody likes to have their words unreasonably dissected. Yet some still do it and then wonder why they have no friends. I have usually disassociated myself from individuals who thought it was their right and even duty to keep me in line and to correct me over petty infractions.

In one church, a woman compiled a list of my preaching errors and approached me after every sermon to bring correction. I put up with it for about three Sundays, when I said, "Stop where you are! Don't ever feel like you have the right to treat me like this." She immediately broke out in tears, saying that her husband harshly and constantly scrutinized her every word and deed. I prayed with her that God would heal her broken heart and help her to righteously and properly confront him. The next week, her husband was murdered by rapid fire from a cartel during a drug deal that turned sour in the Gulf of Mexico. I'm not saying God killed him, but I will say that his arrogance and anger caused his undoing. This dear lady took her offenses out on me until the Lord intervened. Many times individuals who bring offenses need to deal with anger and brokenness in their own life.

Can we start cutting one another slack instead of giving others flack? If a comment or opinion doesn't pertain to our salvation, then leave it alone. Some like to use their Bible knowledge to make others feel "less than." Why embarrass someone or cause a relationship rift over something that simply doesn't matter?

Many offenses occur when people refuse to think twice before they speak once. I've watched many who teach in the areas of healing, the gifts of the Holy Spirit, prosperity, end-time events, and prophetic ministry, especially fall prey to condescending words and judgmental, self-righteous statements that lead to offenses. While these doctrines are wonderful and necessary, those who teach must remember they are held to a higher standard of responsibility.

That's why the apostle James said, "Let not many of you become teachers, my brethren, knowing that as such we will incur a greater judgment" (3:1). Voice tones, perceived rebukes, inflexibility, and poor social skills in general often disqualify those who minister in these sensitive areas of Christian teaching. Such teaching mandates godly wisdom and the ability to communicate clearly and in complete awareness of an audience's current level of understanding. Effective teachers must first gauge their audience to ascertain their knowledge of a given doctrine and then meet them where they're at, not where they think they should be. I've seen many become offended when unwise teachers and preachers addressed their students in a condescending fashion. We who work in Gospel ministry, of all people, need to accurately read our audience. The use of personal examples that elevate "I" need to be tempered when we teach and preach. Even the apostle Paul admitted, "I have not arrived" (Phil. 3:12)!

Offended people lose perspective. How do offenses come into our lives? By turning our hearts away from the Lord. When we take our eyes off Jesus and place them on what people say and do, offenses will surely come. If you look for offenses, you will find them! I personally have witnessed this acceleration throughout my pastoral ministry. The enemy works feverishly to cause God's people to develop hard feelings.

Miscommunications, harsh tones, judgmental statements, gossip, jealousy, competitive attitudes, and a host of other human traits spawn offenses in the hearts of many. To make matters worse, people sometimes allow outside-the-church situations to keep them away. I've heard this said: "I cannot be in the same room with—after what I've seen and heard, and what I know to be true about them." Can we again remember the church is for exactly people like this? Let's demonstrate Christian grace to our community. In one church I pastored, two couples sat in the same pew who had previously been married to one or the other partner. How strange! Both couples chose to move on with their lives and make the best of it. Offenses were put aside and for the sake of their kids and church family, they chose to offer mutual forgiveness. I love being a pastor!

When it comes to offenses, it's the soul that gets offended, not the spirit of a man. Becoming offended is initially not a salvation matter; it's usually the by-product of poor social or communication skills that spew from broken, hurting lives. Add to this reality individuals who cannot receive correction without becoming offended, and you can see why offenses usually cause people to leave churches. Pastors and people in general need to correct sparingly. Usually, the best way is not to say anything!

How many times over the years have I heard, "I won't be back because I got hurt?" Get in line! But let me ask you, "When you get hurt on the job, do you leave?" Or if the bank teller says something insensitive, do you quit banking there? Or if your mom or dad hurt your feelings, do you leave their home, never to return? No, of course not. So why do you recoil when someone at church is less than he or she should be? The setting does not matter. If you hang around people long enough, the potential for getting offended is high! Offenses at church are most unfortunate, but let me say this: I refuse to allow offenses to drive me away from my Lord, my faith community, and potentially into a life of excuse making.

In Psalm 15:1, David asks the question, "Who abides (stays) in God's presence?" He then gives several character issues that if ignored bring instability into our lives. In verse 4, David refers to offenses when he applauds those who "swear to (their) own hurt." In other words, "Those who refuse to allow offenses to hurt them." Blocked offenses keep us from making unwise choices. Absenteeism from the very source instituted by God to help us walk out our faith—the local church—is always the enemy's goal.

For your sake, and God's, don't let offenses drive you away from church and potentially the kingdom. I implore you to keep your eyes on Jesus! As stated earlier, offenses cause soul wounds that involve our mind, will, and emotions. That's why offenses promote perpetual pain. Individuals who become offended can literally carry grudges for years! And we've all heard stories from people who do. Offenses can produce unforgiveness, which in turn, potentially creates bitterness. Now, do you understand why we need to avoid offenses—both giving and receiving them? Offenses have the power to destroy relationships—both with others and Jesus. God forbid!

We need to release our offenders immediately through forgiveness and prayer. Otherwise, we, too, could become the perpetrators of betrayal and hate. Determine not to hold on to offenses when they come. And they will come! One pastor said, "I refuse to be offended." I love his resolve.

Another difficulty arises when we take on the offenses of others. I've seen this happen time and again in the local church. Friends are notorious for taking on one another's offenses. When this happens, the enemy gets two or more for the price of one! I hate it when believers become offended. In my experience, individuals who take on private offenses or the offenses of others more often than not leave churches and even spend the rest of their lives talking about given offenses, like they just happened. Isn't the enemy crafty?

Questions to Ponder

1. Have you ever received or caused an offense at church? Have you made it right?

2. Have you ever taken on the offense(s) of someone else? When?

3. Why are some offenses difficult to let go?

15

Same Song, Same Dance

The local church is not only God's venue to introduce people who are far from him to new life in Jesus Christ, but also help them to mature in their newfound faith. We are called to grow in the grace and knowledge of the Lord. The fact remains, however, that for some people things never change. They choose to become "projects," remaining stuck in the emotional and mental ruts of their past. In a very sick way, they enjoy spinning their tires in the muck and mire of past hurts and life experiences. In short, they are usually drama-driven and spend their time trying to draw everyone else into their sordid, broken world. When they finally realize that people around them tire of hearing repetitive negativity, they become critical and can even become hostile. They either repent of their sinful patterns or they leave.

In my experience, these sad ones usually seek out people just like them with whom they can miserably do life together. In their case, misery surely does breed company! Old habits and attitudes continue to define them. They refuse to acknowledge and repent of those things that become continued fodder for their conversations. They come to church week after week with the intention of picking up where they left off. Verbal exchange is strategically controlled, and they feel threatened when more determined voices override their "same song, same dance" discussions. People like this simply do not understand the appropriateness and courtesy of mutual exchange. It is not uncommon for them to interrupt conversations already in progress. Conversations become all about them. When denied access to listening ears or their comments are subdued by those around them, project people either become more intensely forward or they leave the church. And everyone but them receives the blame.

Instead of recognizing their self-centered, attention-seeking folly, they become more determined to use their emotional pain to launch their ongoing future encounters. And nobody likes or needs a project. And so they leave. This remains their modus operandi and harsh reality. This I find to be sad and as a pastor, I have to guard my heart and those in the local body from being pulled in by such negative individuals. Usually, projects leave local churches when they realize they have exhausted the patience and concern of the overall body. Project people have to be shelved, not highlighted. No one changes who constantly is enabled.

Questions to Ponder

1. Based on the above discussion, am I someone's project?

2. Do I feel guilty avoiding projects? Why or why not?

3. How can I personally help those who tend to wallow in their past?

16

No-Drama Zone

I understand the following discussion closely aligns my treatment on offenses; however, as I look back over my years in ministry, I've seen far too many incidences where individuals simply could not—would not—get along. Like in any family, occasional misunderstandings and squabbles occur between siblings. And sadly enough, individuals leave local churches when they refuse to handle such times according to proper scriptural mandates. And the reason they usually leave is because they refuse to receive correction. One or both refuse to take ownership of their role in the dispute. We often hear "It takes two to tango!" This is true.

In Philippians 4:2–3, Paul very succinctly deals with an apparent squabble between two women in the church:

> I plead with Euodia and I plead with Synteche to be of the same mind in the Lord. Yes, and I ask you, my true companion (Timothy), help those women since they have contended at my side in the cause of the Gospel, along with Clement and the rest of my coworkers, whose names are in this book of life.

Evidently, the fallout between these two women was serious enough for Paul to address in the manner he did. The apostle knew that such dissension could bring church division. Unfortunately, as sick as it may sound, some thrive on drama. Their lives are drama-driven! Details are sketchy, but we do know that both women were leaders in the church at Philippi. He further recognized that both women needed a third party to help them move past their disagreement. They needed an arbitrator.

Yes, saved people at times refuse to die to self when engaged in relationship battles. I read this brief passage, and I think back to times of church division in my pastoral ministry. Unfortunately, some pastors believe the solution rests solely on prayer, and I agree that's a good starting place. Many times, however, such contentions need to be confronted firmly and with tough love. When disagreements escalate beyond resolution, church leaders must take corrective action. Such was the case with Euodia and Synteche.

At Hope Community, I keep my ears to the ground when it comes to church conflict. The enemy (Satan) wants nothing more than to divide the work of God. He has a bag of tricks. One includes individuals becoming offended or at odds with one another. The fallout between Euodia and Synteche was not unlike interpersonal conflicts that take place in today's church. Consider the following observations.

1. Obviously, whatever their bone of contention, Euodia and Synteche were causing churchwide unrest. Two people in conflict may subsequently try to make their problem a church issue. This I guard against tenaciously. They talk to others in the church to build a case in their defense. In Proverbs 6:19, the author relates one of seven things that God hates: "One who sows discord among the brothers." This is not about taking sides; it's about two people owning up to their transgressions and relationship failures.

2. Paul knew that Euodia and Synteche, because of their widespread influence, might look for others to join them in their cause. Nothing good ever comes from taking up the offenses of others. Did you know that all of us carry influence? And did you know that we use our influence

to either hurt or bless the cause of unity? Don't pick up offenses! Instead, pray for restitution among the quarreling parties. And whatever you do, please be careful not to add fuel to the fires of contention. Be a peacemaker, not a troublemaker!

3. We say that Hope Community is a "no-drama church." In other words, we ask people to not take their private issues public. Of course, we want to pray for the needs of people, but we insist that personal issues be taken to the Lord in prayer on a confidential basis. The church lobby, small group, or social media is not the place to perpetuate drama. Some individuals talk too much and tell too much. Daily drama sucks the life out of people and gives the enemy constant access into their situations. I personally despise it when believers use Facebook to air their dirty laundry. Such posting brings reproach on the Gospel. Don't give the devil an opportunity to implode your drama. Are you a "drama queen" or "king?" Then abdicate your throne today!

4. Euodia and Synteche were leaders in the local church. Paul knew that leaders often disqualify themselves from effective ministry when they engage in church division, ongoing drama, or taking up others' offenses. That's why he tells them to "be of the same mind in the Lord." Leaders and people in general often forget that negative perception can disqualify them from future ministry opportunities. Are you a leader? Ask yourself, "How am I perceived by others?"

5. Something in human nature rallies us to immediately take sides when others experience fallout. This is dangerous. When it came to these two women, there was Euodia's truth and then Synteche's truth and then the actual truth! Individuals who determine to get involved in the offenses of others always seem to search for weak links in the church—immature, emotionally broken people—to perpetuate their offenses. We at Hope Community keep our ears open to such shenanigans.

6. Finally, all of us are subject to relationship fallout. Paul's direct appeal to Euodia and Synteche suggests that we are never beyond correction when emotions and tension escalate. We must at all costs protect the integrity of the Gospel. Damage control always becomes necessary when believers refuse to righteously resolve their issues. At Hope Community, we watch and pray against such goings-on and are determined to confront anything that hurts the forward momentum God has given us.

Another side note: All local churches have potential "Euodia and Synteche" situations. However, damage control is more difficult in the smaller church because of more potential close-knit relationships. Individuals easily tend to turn their feelings inwardly. It becomes all too easy for God's people to judge and criticize others. If left unsupervised, people literally devour one another! Smaller local churches particularly fall prey to petty squabbles and quickly become toxic environments. This must be safeguarded at all costs.

Questions to Ponder

1. Do I know of anyone in my church who struggles to get along with others? Have I prayed for him or her?

2. Have I ever taken up the offenses of those I love?

3. What lessons do I personally learn from Euodia and Synteche's squabble?

4. Have I ever fought with someone in my church? Have I made it right?

17

First Earn the Right

It never ceases to amaze me—frustrate me—when people come into the local church and become self-appointed critics. While virtually unknown, some even set out to change what they don't like or disagree with. And sometimes they do it boldly and without tact. In short, they rub everyone the wrong way. People learn to tolerate critics; that is, until they can't stand anymore! It amazes me when newcomers automatically feel it their right, even responsibility, to criticize the building, the service structure, the pastor's message, and other things.

For example, a man visited our service when we were undergoing renovations, and when I greeted him, the first thing he said was, "You need to get covers on two electrical outlets in the sanctuary. This is very dangerous." While what he said may have been true, the fact that he said it made me suspect of his motivations. I marked him on the spot as potential trouble and immediately did not like him! I'm sure my body language said so. Honestly, I was not sad when he never returned. Another man, minutes after his arrival, pulled me aside and said, "The music is too loud, and the song selection does not fit your service structure." I kindly, with gritted teeth, asked him to have a seat. Later, he said, "This church is not for me." I couldn't have agreed more!

Where do critics get off? Do they not understand that what they're doing is sowing discord? These people fail to understand the necessity of first gaining the trust of the pastor or church family, nor do they understand an all-important principle that guides healthy interactions: We must first earn the right before we speak into other's lives—in this case, the church's functions. No one likes a critic who unfortunately becomes branded and labeled as trouble! After a period of self-righteous isolation, they typically feel unwelcome and leave. Critics would not have to leave if they would lighten up, walk in wisdom, and become part of the solution, not part of the problem.

Questions to Ponder

1. Am I ever unduly critical? If so, how? What measures do I need to take to stop being critical?

2. Are there critics in my church? If so, what can I do to help redirect them?

3. In what way do critics sow discord?

18

Throw Her Out the Window

$\mathcal{D}$o you remember the story of Jezebel in the Old Testament? It is recorded in both 1 and 2 Kings. She was King Ahab's wife, the queen mother. This ungodly woman promoted the worship of false gods in Israel, harassed and killed God's prophets, and arranged for an innocent man to be falsely charged and executed (1 Kings 21). King Ahab allowed his wife to emasculate him. He actually lived in fear of her and allowed her to use her evil influence to bring deceit, destruction, and death to innocent lives. Ahab was a spineless man who should never have married Jezebel in the first place, much less allowed her to carry on her evil rampages. Theirs was an unholy alliance.

I firmly believe that Satan, the archenemy of the local church, places Jezebel plants inside churches today. I know because I have pastored some of them! The Jezebel spirit, if left unchecked, has the ability to bring great harm to churches. This spirit is deceptive in its approach, controlling and usually loud. It majors on intimidation tactics. Often, individuals who operate under a Jezebel spirit work behind the scenes to recruit weak links in the church. What constitutes a weak link? Anyone who lacks spiritual discernment, who is easily swayed, and who desperately yearns for friends—even controlling ones—readily falls prey to Jezebel spirits. Jezebel seeks out and preys on broken lives who gladly but unknowingly submit to her evil advances.

Eventually, birds of a feather flock together, and the end result is innocent, precious lives caught up in confusion and strife. Jezebel must be ousted in order to bring peace. "Then he (Jehu the king) lifted up his face to the window and said, 'Who is on my side? Who?' And two or three officials looked down at him. He said, 'Throw her down.' So they threw her down, and some of her blood was sprinkled on the wall and on the horses, and he trampled her under foot" (2 Kings 9:32–33). Damage control must happen at times in the local church for the sake of the whole. Pastors who allow such individuals to freely roam wild in the church pay a terrible price for their unwillingness to confront. Men can possess a Jezebel spirit, but usually, it's women who operate in this demonic realm. What are some leading characteristics of a Jezebel spirit?

- It is deceptive, often masquerading as a caring, supportive presence.
- It loves to control people, situations, and ministries.
- At first it seems plausible, but given time, it reveals itself as divisive.
- It detests and even hates spiritual authority, refusing to submit to instructions and of course, correction.
- It always tries to build a following.
- It most always hates male leadership and male authority, often overriding spousal leadership in the home.
- It is a lying, deceiving spirit.
- It often tries to hide behind pseudo-spiritual words and actions, thus making accurate pastoral discernment a "must."
- When confronted, it becomes hateful and belligerent.
- It seldom repents and has to be tossed out (read 2 Kings 9:30–37 to get the whole story). Casting out Jezebel is a good thing and pastors need to act swiftly and without apology. When Jezebel leaves the local church, tension leaves with her, and peace is restored. Everyone rejoices. We could care less if Jezebel says goodbye. Good riddance!

Questions to Ponder

1. Do I support my pastor when a Jezebel spirit has to be confronted and cast out in my local church?

2. Do I guard against a Jezebel spirit trying to influence me?

3. Do I use the influence God gives me to build my church and never tear it down?

4. Do I righteously and secretly pray against any evil influence that tries to invade my church?

19

Trouble in Paradise

"*These* six things the Lord hates. Yes, seven are an abomination to Him: A proud look, a lying tongue, hands that shed innocent blood, a heart that devises wicked plans, feet that are swift in running to evil, a false witness who speaks lies, and *one who sows discord among brethren*" (Prov. 6:16–19). To sow discord is to say and do things that cause strife among one another. Local churches must take definitive action when such strife surfaces. Usually the "sower" acts as if he or she is not trying to cause arguments. Sowing discord is something done in secret, and that's what makes it so potentially lethal. God describes it as an abomination because it leads to division. God hates it because he loves unity.

When an individual engages in sowing discord, he aligns with the enemy. Sowing discord is a serious offense for the believer. Those who engage in this act must be confronted quickly and decisively. Pastors need to have their facts straight and keep their heart pure, so as to avoid a kangaroo court. Predetermined conclusions have no place. Second Corinthians 13:1 establishes the godly procedure for these heart-wrenching times in local church ministry: "In the mouths of two to three witnesses, let these things be established." This may be an ancient law, but it strives to attain righteous results.

Such meetings must always be held in private. Believers, regardless of their position during these meetings, should practice mutual respect. Emotions, regardless how potentially runaway, must be tucked under the blood of Jesus and times, places, words spoken, and accurate details should be well documented. Unfortunately, I've never been part of a clear-cut session to expose those who unashamedly sow discord. It usually ends up his word, her word, and the right word! These times are never easy in the life of a local church. However, if discord is not confronted, the church could face ruin. Lying, gossip, fault-finding, hate, disrespect, false accusations, anger, and other works of the flesh cannot be tolerated. Of course, genuine repentance is the desired outcome by all parties involved; however, in my experience, complete restoration is seldom the outcome. Sowing discord is a canker in the life of any church. The sooner it is dealt with, the better. A good reputation is the church's best friend, both in the community and within its doors. Like with individuals, a soiled reputation is a difficult reality to overcome. Again, that's why pastors must deal promptly and decisively when there's trouble in paradise!

Otherwise, the more time that is allowed to pass, the more unscrupulous minds take opportunities to spread their venom. Damage control must be enforced. Personal feelings cannot be the determining factor. The church at large must be the overriding concern. Yes, people will probably leave, but godly leaders must count the costs in order to build healthy churches. Sowing discord is one of the devil's greatest attacks on the local church. If left unchecked, churches suffer setbacks that sometimes take years to stabilize. I have pastored six churches and witnessed various levels of discord in each one. All such upheaval began in secret and pushed its way into the body life of the church.

Here's the thing: Nobody handles these times with complete success. The bottom line in church dissension is pride. The preacher calls it a "proud look" (Prov. 6:16). Another translation describes it as a "haughty spirit." Either way, pride is a fierce contender. The apostle Paul possessed a pastor's heart, but readily exposed individuals who sowed discord in his ministry. In 2 Timothy 4:14, we read, "Alexander the Coppersmith (metal worker) did me much harm. May the Lord repay him according to his works. You also must be aware of him, for he has greatly resisted our words." We, of course, are not given specifics, but we can easily suppose that Alexander followed Paul about, telling lies, creating division, and resisting the man of God.

Can I be honest? Ministry is hard enough without putting up with this kind of behavior. The enemy loves to oppose the work of God and always finds a broken, carnal, even bitter vessel to employ his divisive tactics. These individuals matter to the Lord, but their ungodly conduct cannot be allowed to go unchecked in the family of God.

Have I handled church discord well over the years? I'm not going to mislead you. Church discord has taken me to the limit, literally costing me two churches. If only I could do it all over again! Well, not really! But if we pastors can learn from our mistakes and shortcomings, then we are one step ahead. At Hope Community, I keep my ear to the ground and try to head off at the pass any hints of church discord. I am known by most as a kind, caring and merciful man. However, when individuals sow discord, people see a much different side of me. And many ask, "What's going on with Pastor Roger?" My answer is simple: "There are wolves among the flock, and they must be exposed and driven out."

Pastor friend, there are times when we don't have to be nice! "The kingdom of God suffers violence and the violent must take it by force" (Matt. 11:12). This verse references John the Baptist who understood that his ministry would be misunderstood! Jesus was pointing out the immense persecution resulting from the Gospel of the kingdom being preached. Satan was putting up quite a fight to keep Israel in spiritual blindness. Herod would soon have John beheaded. In the meantime, John would take a bold stand as forerunner of the Messiah. John was courageous and certainly not "seeker friendly." He never allowed public opinion to sideline his message. And so it is when pastors have to use their influence to correct impending discord in the life of the church.

Questions to Ponder

1. Why must church discord be stamped out ASAP?

2. "Hands that shed innocent blood" refers to murder. How does this phrase pertain to sowing discord?

3. What types of people do those who sow discord prey upon?

20

When Johnny Can't Read

$\mathcal{I}$ have a theory. The Scriptures declare that Satan is a master strategist: "In order that Satan might not outwit us, for we are not unaware of his schemes" (2 Cor. 2:11). Another translation says, "We are not ignorant of his devices." However, I'm not sure about that. I think we as a church culture have been ignorant or at least lured into a subtle sleep. And it has to do with Johnny not being able to read. Let me explain.

In 1955 best-selling author, Rudolf Flesch, wrote a book entitled *Why Johnny Can't Read*. This book attacked the discontinuance of phonics to teach children to read. Later *Time* magazine would ask the same question when reading levels continued to substantially decline across the country. In 1983, Flesch wrote the sequel, *Why Johnny Still Can't Read*, continuing his campaign to reform reading in America.

Over the years I've heard Christian leaders say, "Satan is stupid, he's a defeated foe." However, this is only partially true. Yes, Jesus defeated Satan on the Cross, winning over death and hell. But the consummation of that victory will not be fully realized until Jesus returns and Satan is ultimately cast into the Lake of Fire (Rev. 20:10). In the meantime, the battle for men's souls continues to rage. Individuals are still called upon to make Christ their Savior and Lord, and because we still live on this fallen planet, the consummation of all things still lies ahead. So the previous statement represents only partial truth.

Satan is a lot of things, but "stupid" is not one of them. The Scriptures tell us, "Faith comes by hearing and hearing by the words of Christ" (Rom. 10:17). Christianity has always been a "religion of the Book." The Bible, when read and acted upon, transforms the human spirit. Other books inform and perhaps conform the way we think, but only the Bible transforms the heart of man. Jesus declares, "The words I have spoken to you are full of the Spirit and they bring life" (John 6:63).

I personally believe the reason Johnny can't read is because the enemy secretly, subtly, and with prolonged determination undermined the educational system of this country. The proof is in the pudding. Reading skills have continued to decline ever since the use of phonics was removed from our elementary schools. I thank God that I attended a school that embraced the use of phonics in the 1960s. I was taught to read in small groups where phonics helped us sound out difficult words.

What's my point? When reading skills decline, Bible reading or any reading for that matter is shelved for lesser pursuits. When Johnny no longer reads, the written words of Christ are unable to bring life-changing results. I was alarmed when I recently heard a man raised in the 1970s say, "I never learned to read, and I hate to read. I have no desire to read the Bible." At first I thought, "How sad." Then, the further reality of his statement set off an alarm in my spirit. That's one way Satan undermines Christian endeavor today. When believers don't like to read, or can't read, they place in jeopardy their ability to grow to maturity. Again, Satan may be defeated; however, he is anything but stupid!

When Johnny can't read, he is unable to draw from the life-sustaining words of Christ that save and mature him in his faith. This remains a cause for concern! And local churches will invariably suffer loss. Pastors, if I may, allow me to recommend remedial reading classes as part of your church's outreach program. Unusual? Yes! Necessary? I think so! Also, you may want to encourage your people to buy a *Message Bible* or one of the many other easier to read Bible versions available today. The *King James Version* and other translations may prove difficult for those who struggle with reading skills and comprehension.

Are you the parent of a preschooler? Let me encourage you to make reading a priority in your home. You may want to turn off the television, lay aside the cell phone, disengage Alexa and video games, and make good books available for your children. Buy a good children's Bible, read along with them, and make reading fun. Grandparents, too, can help impart life skills! Good reading skills will produce eternal results!

Questions to Ponder

1. What important correlation exists between the success of the local church and good reading skills?

2. How do poor reading skills factor in Christian growth and maturity?

3. Why might someone who reads poorly see church as optional?

21

Blinds, Binds, and Grinds

Many years ago, an acquaintance of mine who struggled with alcohol and suffered from cirrhosis of the liver said to me, "I don't believe in sin. We control our own destiny." She vehemently refused to acknowledge sin's hold on her life and later died a terribly painful death. Iniquity issues blinded her to the truth. While writing *Monday Morning Preacher*, I conducted a man on the street interview, asking the question, "What is sin?" Here's what I heard in part:

"Sin is breaking the Ten Commandments" (elderly woman).
"Sin is being bad" (little girl).
"Sin is highlighted when the church shames and guilts people" (young man).
"I don't have a clue" (teenage girl).
"Sin is killing people" (man in his twenties).
"Sin is whatever 'p—God off'" (elderly man).
"Sin is what makes people do terrible things" (middle-aged woman).

Perhaps we all need to rethink the definition of sin because I believe that many who pass through local churches leave needlessly and without a biblical understanding of what sin really is, and its impact on the world, nations, homes, and individuals. To preach or teach about sin without providing a way out is almost cruel. Talk about hopeless! When I was a preteen, I heard a sermon about the effects of sin based on the life of Samson taken from Judges 16:21, "Then the Philistines seized him and gouged out his eyes, and they brought him down to Gaza and bound him with bronze chains, and he was a grinder in the prison." I remember the outline like it was yesterday:

I.   Sin blinds.
II. Sin binds.
III. Sin grinds.

And then, the service ended. I left feeling bewildered! I learned what sin did to Samson, and what it does to all of us, but what I did not hear was how I could be released from sin's hold in my life. I still compare that message to when a parent spanks a child for doing something bad, then says "Now, tell me you love me!" Talk about mixed emotions! Thank God that Jesus is the remedy for the sin problem. "He who bore our sins in His body on the tree" (1 Pet. 2:24) provides a way of escape. That outline lacked a major component—an ending! That unfinished sermon needed a whizbang conclusion! Points I, II, and III were fine, but they presented the problem without providing a solution. Thank God that Jesus is point IV. Because of his shed blood, sin no longer has dominion over us!

Let's face it. Some people leave churches because they hear about God's righteous standards but never embrace the imputed righteousness of Jesus. Over time, they allow the reality of sin to cloud their understanding and keep them away. Hearing the preached Word brings conviction, and the anointing terrorizes them! I feel strongly that we need to expand our teaching about sin to include iniquities and transgressions. We have victory over sins, iniquities, and transgressions through the blood of Jesus! Psalm 32:1–5 says,

> How blessed is he whose *transgression* is forgiven, whose *sin* is covered! How blessed is the man to whom the Lord does not impute *iniquity*. And in whose spirit there is no deceit. When I

kept silent about my *sin*, my body wasted away, through my groaning all day long. For day and night Your hand was heavy upon me. My vitality was drained away as with the fervent heat of summer. I acknowledged my *sin* to You, and my *iniquity* did not hide. I said, "I will confess my *transgressions* to the Lord, and you will forgive the guilt of my *sin*."

Obviously, the Bible writer differentiates between sins, iniquities, and transgressions. And a clear understanding of these differences may help individuals grasp their faith in a different, more-encompassing way. When we talk only about sin and ignore the reality of transgressions and iniquities, we may heap unnecessary, unhealthy guilt upon our listeners. Without explaining the cause and effect of sin's hold on our lives, we may very well place saved people under a "why try" mind-set. I remember in my youth leaving church and saying, "I'll never be good enough to serve the Lord." I'll discuss this more at length when I discuss legalism. A sad reality is that many leave our churches because they either don't want to repent, or they may have repented and still struggle with sin's effects, thus misunderstanding the hold that transgressions and iniquities have in their lives.

For them we pray, asking the Lord to draw them into a healthy, balanced Christian experience. We yearn for the day when they allow sin's hold to let go and find new life in Christ. These family members remain a constant concern, and when they leave, we continue to pray for them. Only prayer can turn their hearts to the Lord! I firmly believe I'm in the kingdom of God today because of a praying grandmother and pastors who knew how to intercede for the lost. How I thank God for those who wept over me instead of continually judging my behavior. They loved me unconditionally.

Let me ask you a question. What is the purpose of the local church? Why does it exist? Our vision statement at Hope Community says in part, "We exist so that people who are far from God find new life in Christ." This statement suggests two very basic truths: (1) The church is not a club for saints, but a hospital for broken and hurting people, and (2) salvation is both instantaneous and progressive.

In other words, we should not expect new believers to be perfect. In fact, we cannot expect perfection from anyone! The church is not for perfect people. Church marquee commonly read: "Perfect people not allowed!" We often, however, forget that broken humanity is our target audience, and we should not feel it necessary to stand in judgment. As a matter of fact, if we waited to get our act together before we were good enough to go to church, we'd never get there! Some local churches actually become uncomfortable when newcomers enter their doors. I know this sounds ridiculous, but local churches who forget about their mission to win the lost easily become hidden behind closed doors, now members of an exclusive club for the spiritually elite. In essence, they become self-contained. How many people have left churches because they did not feel good enough to be there? Yes, we're all sinners who need to get hooked up with the Savior, and yes, we all fall short. But it remains paramount that we never forget our reason for being.

I still remember Pastor Tommy Barnett, former pastor of First Assembly, Phoenix, Arizona (now Dream City Church) saying many years ago, "Our church parking lots should be full of cigarette butts!" Church programs and ways of doing things are fine—that is, if they don't cater to the already saved and forget that broken, hurting people can actually feel excluded—not good enough. In my experience, churches quit growing when they turn their eyes inwardly, and quit looking on the "fields that are ready for harvest" (John 4:35). People who are yet far from God should feel accepted and genuinely loved when they enter church doors. There should be no difference in treatment shown between saint and sinner.

On the heels of this, God's people would do well to remember that all of us are hopelessly broken and undone apart from Jesus Christ. And that hurt people hurt people. Broken people tend to gossip, speak negatively of others, and even lie about one another. This, of course, is a terrible reality, and one that mandates believers to speak only well of one another. But the sad fact is they sometimes don't. How sinful and unrighteous we can be!

These harsh realities have always caused people to leave churches, and I'm sure the Father's heart is broken over such ungodly conduct. Don't forget. Local churches cooperate with the Holy Spirit to instill the progressive work of grace into the lives of faithful attendees. Faithful, uninterrupted attendance, and sitting under the preaching of God's Word progressively transforms all of us more and more into the image of Jesus Christ—if we mix it with faith. "For unto us was the gospel preached as well as unto them; but the word which they heard did not profit them, not being mixed with faith in those who heard it" (Heb. 4:2).

Questions to Ponder

1. Do I regularly pray for the lost?

2. Do I continually remind myself about the local church's reason for being?

3. How do I make unbelievers feel when they're around me? Do they feel uncomfortable or repelled by my words and/ or actions?

4. Do I have a healthy understanding of what sin really is?

22

Just Different Faces

$\mathscr{L}$egalism, or the excessive adherence to law, or stressing obedience apart from faith, infiltrated the Church from its infancy. The apostle Paul confronted its devastating impact, especially in Romans and Galatians. It's not a new problem. It just takes on different faces. And it's a harsh motivator to live for Christ.

Many who grew up in the 1950s and '60s were frequently exposed to legalistic preaching. Of course, there are still many pockets of this type of preaching in today's church. My personal experience in the legalistic community hails from local churches that embraced Wesleyan theology. In short, this included Pentecostal churches, holiness churches, and off-shoots of these two. They were not bad people; in fact, they were wonderful in their own right. They simply embraced a works-oriented theology (Armenian) and felt the only way to make heaven their eventual home was by working hard to please God.

Before I move on, let me define Armenian theology versus Calvinistic theology, which represent two opposite camps of thought on the subject of salvation. Armenians place a strong emphasis on our personal role while Calvinists stress God's role. In other words, both camps attempt to explain how one gets to heaven. Armenians place much emphasis on personal performance, and Calvinists talk a lot about "irresistible grace." This teaches that God's grace to save a person cannot be resisted.

This means that if God gives grace to you, there is nothing in the world that can resist it and thwart God's intention to take you to heaven. Someone described it this way: "We get dragged kicking and screaming into heaven!" To summarize (perhaps an oversimplification), some say we get to heaven on our own merits, and others say we will arrive strictly because of what Jesus Christ did for us on the Cross. Each camp differs in its view of sanctification, but both viewpoints admit that it requires faith. As for me, I'm somewhere in the middle, but that's another book!

Regardless of where you may fit in this theological continuum, legalistic preaching is found at some level in most all theological persuasions. This type of preaching usually employs shame and unhealthy guilt to get their point across. And many times, the reality of a physical hell is held over listeners' heads to fully emphasize the absolute necessity of living right. Is hell a real place? Absolutely. The Scriptures describe it as a literal place. Who goes to hell? All who reject Jesus Christ. However, we may need to so adamantly quit scaring "hell out of people" and preach that it's the "kindness (goodness) of God that leads men to repentance" (Rom. 2:4). Fear is a harsh motivator that eventually causes people to react negatively.

I totally agree with what Pastor Steven Furtick from Elevation Church says. "Most churches today are known for what they don't like or disagree with, instead of what they like and agree with." The church in America, in many sectors, has perhaps presented a negative image to an unbelieving culture. We have consistently used negative methods to present earth's most positive message! Law-based preaching exposes sin without providing a positive way out. Grace-filled preaching exposes sin and provides a means of escape. The first makes it impossible to live right; the second may make it too easy. Law-based preaching makes people want to give up and quit trying. Imbalanced grace preaching insinuates that God has gone soft on sin. May God help us strike a balance.

My friend, determine to live as closely to the Lord as you can and as he reveals himself in his Word. Remember, "The Law came through Moses, but grace and truth came through Jesus Christ" (John 1:17). God gave the law to show us our need for a Savior.

Grace shows us Jesus, the way out of our sin! Too many have left local churches because of a "rules and regulations" religious mentality. Remember further, that serving Jesus Christ is not about religion; it's about a relationship of the saving kind. Don't let a misunderstanding of law versus grace keep you from enjoying the wonders of belonging to a local church.

I promised earlier I would briefly discuss sin as it pertains to iniquities and transgressions. I'm convinced that most people have an incomplete understanding of what sin is, and so they struggle with the ongoing effects of sin in their daily lives. Post-conversion issues prove that sin's hold on all of us is stronger than we fully realize. Add legalistic preaching to the mix, and it's no small wonder why many are on their way to heaven, but not enjoying the trip! Church services ought to be the most enjoyable time of our week. When we understand what iniquities and transgressions are, hopefully we will live balanced Christian lives that bring joy to the Lord and peace to our souls. Legalism will lose its hold! Before you proceed, go back, and read Psalm 32:1–5 (under the sin discussion in chapter 21).

So what are iniquities? Predispositions to certain sins (usually morality based) constitute iniquities. These predispositions often try to resurface after we come to faith in Christ. Hence, the phrase "post-conversion issues." Some refer to these struggles as generational issues that try to pull us down. Some Bible teachers refer to iniquities as generational curses. For example, in my family background, alcohol is an iniquity issue. Praise God, it was broken out of my life when I accepted Jesus Christ as my personal Savior in 1970. But sadly, alcoholism was rampant in the paternal side of our family, going back at least three generations. I can't stand the taste of alcohol, so that discouraged me from indulging! However, others in the family swore up and down they hated the effects of alcohol, and that they would never touch the stuff. Today, some of them are alcoholics because they were no match for iniquity's stronghold. Only the blood of Jesus cancels out iniquity's power.

I cringe when I hear Christians who struggled with alcohol or other addictive behaviors prior to their salvation place themselves in potentially compromising situations. For instance, believers who have a predisposition to abuse alcohol need not visit places where alcohol is served. They toy with the devil! Whatever God delivers you from should be avoided.

Ask Samson, Israel's playboy-prophet, if you don't understand. From his youth, this strongman apparently had a problem with lust. When he got older, he consorted with a prostitute who used her lust-filled prowess to bring him down. Israel's judge was no match for his iniquity—propensity to entertain lustful stimuli—and it made a buffoon out of him. In today's world, notably during COVID-19, many bored men who previously struggled with internet porn are falling prey to online sites that showcase their folly. Guys who more than usual struggle with the pull of lust (iniquity) need to either stay away from the internet or download porn blockers. Really, males in general need to avoid internet folly. Being alone without accountability is never smart, as again, this iniquity issue is no match for the fallen nature.

What are transgressions? In our "Lord's Prayer," we ask him to "forgive us our trespasses, as we forgive those who trespass against us" (Matt. 6:14). The word *trespass* and the word *transgressions* are similar. They both deal with relationships. All of us, if we're honest, leave a trail of broken relationships behind us. Nowhere is the fallen nature more obvious or poignant than in the area of relationships. When Adam and Eve fell by way of transgression, relationships were the hardest hit. First and foremost, our relationship with God was broken, and that, in turn, caused all earthly relationships to be compromised by sin. Saved people need to understand the dynamics of the new birth as it pertains to iniquities and transgressions. First, understand that salvation is an event that is worked out in process. When we reduce sin to a list of "can't dos," we forfeit the whole spectrum of sanctification. The sanctifying work of the Holy Spirit is worked out as we surrender the various "kingdoms of our heart" to the Lord.

Sin, as the legalist defines it, includes a list of "no-nos" the Christian must avoid in order to be truly saved. When I was a young believer, the list included no dancing, smoking, chewing tobacco, drinking alcoholic beverages, attending movie theaters, no pants on women, no country music, and others too numerous to remember. However, when our definition of sin goes no deeper, most find they cannot live according to certain standards, and they feel inadequate and become easily discouraged. Many give up in frustration.

Often, well-meaning Christians who truly love the Lord live in guilt and shame because they never match up to man-made regulations. They in essence feel like they'll never be good enough for God to accept. Interestingly, the "sin list" presented by each religious persuasion often differs from church to church. It took me years to understand that ongoing iniquity and transgression issues drove me to hide in shame. I did not understand that the "bigger sins" were often symptomatic of soul wounds. If only someone would have told me to renew my mind by the Word of God (Eph. 4:23).

Now, you can understand why there's so much confusion in legalistic-driven churches and so much fallout. Remember, Christian friend, you are not saved because you live according to a prescribed set of rules and regulations. You are not saved because you obey the Ten Commandments. You are not saved because of your good works, but you are saved to do good works! You are saved because you have placed your faith and trust in the precious blood of Jesus. You do not have righteousness; you are righteousness! He (God) now looks at you through the blood of his Son and declares you to be 100 percent righteous. "He (God) made Him (Jesus), who knew no sin, to be sin, on our behalf, so that we might become the righteousness of God in Him" (2 Cor. 5:21). The indwelling Spirit then gives you the power to live a holy life as you surrender your iniquities and transgressions to him! He's so wonderful!

Questions to Ponder

1. What does it mean to be legalistic?

2. Why does legalism not satisfy a searching heart?

3. What are the differences between sin, transgressions, and iniquities?

4. Be honest, if only privately. What iniquities and/or transgressions are you struggling with?

5. What is your personal understanding of Armenian versus Calvinistic theology?

23

Too Many Choices

Have you noticed an acceleration of choices in our culture? I sure have! I personally believe Satan has masterminded a subtle yet strategic mind-set designed to encourage "busyness" and to keep people stressed out. Busyness leads to barrenness, where individuals become emotionally and mentally tired, thus making them unproductive. Fun things can also wear people down. We were not created to "go, go, go." Even God rested on the seventh day! I heard evangelist Benny Hinn say many years ago, "The world emphasizes 'enjoy,' while God's emphasis is simply 'joy.'" And yet many today find themselves in a rat-race of stress-filled living. To seek out only enjoyment in life is perhaps another drug of choice.

Some of our stress is not work-related but rather pleasure-related. The prophet Daniel said the day would come when "many would run to and fro" (12:4). We've arrived! I personally believe we should enjoy life and engage in fun activities, but we still need to strike a balance. If either enjoyment or work become our priorities and consistently steal us away from God's house, we need to put the brakes on. Most activities can wait until Sunday afternoon, and if they can't, perhaps we need to rethink our decisions. One family said to me, "It's summertime and that means camping season is here." Pastor, we'll probably see you in September." Part of me thought they were kidding. However, I never saw them again. My friend, the enemy knows how to gradually steal our affections away from the house of God. Don't let temporal pursuits override matters of eternal significance. Occasional weekend getaways may be fine, but allowing work and pleasure to consistently steal your affections away from the local church may cost you more than you're willing to pay. This leads me to discuss blue laws.

What are blue laws? Individuals born after 1985 probably have not heard about them. The term "blue law" refers to the prohibiting of alcohol sales on Sunday. It is historically a body of regulations designed to preserve the Sabbath by proscribing most labor on that day. The closing of retail and other business venues was also common. Without sounding maudlin, I miss the innocence of those days. My mind's eye just conjured up a famous Andy Griffith television scene. I saw Aunt Bea, Andy, and Barney sitting on the front porch, passing time away on a lazy Mayberry Sunday afternoon. Church and dinner were over, and homemade ice cream was the topic of discussion. To tell you the truth, that appeals to me right now! But let's stay in the moment!

Culture, it seems, is no longer friendly toward the local church. As a matter of fact, it has become quite competitive with the community of faith. When I was growing up, church services were held in high respect, at least in the smaller communities. As a matter of fact, sports events, whether sponsored by schools or communities, were never held on Sunday mornings. And I also remember that many times schools even refused to schedule sports events on Wednesday evenings, as many churches held midweek services. Little League baseball, other sports events, Boy and Girl Scouts and other community organizations also respected the role of the church, remembering its time-honored service traditions. But not today.

Competitive mind-sets, pleasure seekers, and spiritually subversive community and school leaders, along with retail owners now vie for Sunday morning time slots. Schools tend to minimize the role that local churches play in the lives of our youth, and community activities often conflict with church service schedules. Alcohol outlets, once prohibited from selling on Sunday, now open their doors to welcome their multimillion-dollar consumer industry. Sunday sales now also occur in retail stores and many other types of businesses. Some minimize church attendance, exchanging the eternal for the temporal. I'm concerned. Call me old-fashioned, but with most churches now having only Sunday morning services, I feel I have a right to be!

The church world has surrendered so much and our culture has paid so much in the process. May God give the local church accelerated favor in this, a monumentally difficult time in history. And may believers everywhere quit looking for reasons to give up on earth's greatest enterprise—the local church!

Questions to Ponder

1. What, if anything, is Satan using to steal your affections away from God's house?

2. Have you noticed an acceleration of choices in culture? Explain.

3. How can seeking out pleasure become another "drug of choice"?

4. If you are over forty-five years old, what do you specifically remember about "blue law" days?

5. What's your take on most churches now having only Sunday morning services?

6. What can godly parents do to counteract the propensity of communities to schedule sports events on Sunday mornings?

24

Don't Be Churchy

It may sound funny to some, and even contradictory when I say the family unit has become, in many cases, adversarial toward the local church. I have taught for years that in order of priority, we should place God first in our lives and then family and then church. And often this teaching has come back to bite me in my good intentions. I still believe this order to be right; however, families who look for alternatives to church attendance sometimes use my words to justify their absence from the house of God. Family outings, sports events, weekend excursions, reunions, hiking, amusement parks, and other Sunday events have summoned believers to abuse what I still believe to be God's priority order. Please let me explain what I now see as a juxtaposition.

In days gone by, some well-meaning parents used the local church for punitive reasons. What do I mean? Attendance at church functions in those homes was nonnegotiable. When the church doors were open, everyone in the family was not only expected but demanded to attend. Homework, Little League baseball, school events—band, sports, clubs, proms, field trips—were suspended without apology, and sadly, many youth especially grew to resent the inflexibility of such decisions. You know, it's tough raising parents! Perhaps there are times when church activities need to be put on hold so that our children can lead balanced spiritual and social lives. Everyone needs getaway time. And family vacations create memories for years to come. But these times need to be the exception, never the rule. Let me further explain.

I differentiate between God and church because it has been all too easy for families to become "churchy" without truly loving the Lord and making church a life sentence instead of wholly loving him and serving him through the local church. Using the church to steal fun times and bring discipline, even punishment to children, is unwise.

I have talked with good people over the years who grew up in homes where church attendance overrode the need for family members, and specifically teenagers, to experience a healthy social life, which left a bad taste in their mouth toward church involvement. How sad! Do you see what I'm talking about? When I say, God, family, and church, I'm referring to a balanced lifestyle that says, "We are Christians, and we will serve the Lord through our local church. And on occasion, we will take time away—even Sundays—to enjoy one another, to build family love and unity, all the while wondering what was happening in our wonderful church in our absence!" Do you get what I'm saying? *Yes*, take time away. *No*, don't use the church to inadvertently build walls in your kid's lives. Pray that they grow up to love and serve Jesus. And encourage them always to love and support the local church with their attendance, their resources, and the gifts inside them.

Questions to Ponder

1. How do parents potentially make their children view the church in a negative light?

2. Why does the author differentiate between placing God first and then the local church?

3. What does a balanced lifestyle produce?

25

Times Have Changed

When I compare 2021 to 1960, the differences are many and the similarities are almost nonexistent. The past six decades have brought a whirlwind of change. Honestly, I miss the simpler, more innocent days of my childhood. But guess what? I'm never getting them back, so I have no choice but to live in the present and enjoy today. Perhaps like you, I know people who choose to live in the past, and they're no fun to be around. With them, today always comes up short! How many of us have glorified our past because of fuzzy memories? An occasional visit to yesteryear may be fine, but those who choose to get stuck there waste the precious moments that today brings.

In much the same way, local churches many times refuse to change their methods, fearing the message might become diluted. Many equate changes in methodology with compromise. We must remember that while methods are subject to ongoing change, our message is nonnegotiable and eternal. On the other hand, some churches, unbelievably, have not changed their methods for decades.

Some months ago, I stopped at a country church to meet the pastor. I had to walk through the sanctuary to find the pastor's office. And there it was! An attendance board hung on the front wall—a relic of the 1960s. I had flashbacks to my boyhood church. I laughed out loud before I caught myself, and then a sense of sadness swept over me. Why do we refuse to adapt to contemporary culture without calling it compromise? I suppose that attendance boards created momentum in their day. I'm sure people loved the weekly con-trast-comparison factors! However, its use is outdated in a day when people give online and by texting specific numbers! Fight it, and you could potentially rob yourself of better methods now available!

Later, the pastor informed me the church was 120 years old, and the current medium congregant age was seventy-two. My heart sank! "We have no children or youth," the elderly pastor continued. By her own admission, the church was likely to close its doors in the near future. Then, what I heard next told the tale. "We have stood our ground," she said. "We sing only hymns with the piano, and we do not allow coffee or food in the church like so many others are doing. We give God our best on Sundays—ties and coats on the men and dresses only on the women." She tried twice to pull me into her way of thinking! "Don't you agree?" she asked. Such thinking and approach to ministry has spelled their impending demise. These "little-big" issues mark the difference between perpetuity or dying a slow death.

Several years ago, a Sunday visit took me to another country church where the few in attendance sang "Happy Birthday" (church version) to those celebrating during that month. The pastor stood at the front of the sanctuary for what seemed like hours, begging those with birthdays to come forward and place their offering in a white, plastic church. Finally, he took change out of his own pocket and gave it to an obviously embarrassed little girl. The whole ordeal took at least fifteen minutes. That shy child who fought back tears was forced to walk up front by who I believed to be her grandmother. The child may have grown up viewing the church in a negative light. I hope not. Again, another method that needs to be placed in church archives.

What we emphasize in ministry methodology either brings perpetuity or death. Perpetuity is strangulated or assured, depend-ing on how each new generation views essentials versus nonessen-tials. Nonessentials, when concreted in the minds of inflexible, per-haps well-meaning people—church leaders—usually kill any future momentum. The really sad part of this is when people give God credit for their misgivings. I drove away from both churches, fighting back tears. How can basically good people embrace such a closed mind?

Changing times call for changing methods. You would think common sense would dictate this reality, much less the discernment of the Holy Spirit. And sadly, some leave churches due to their irrelevant methods. Perhaps you remember *Little House on the Prairie*, which aired on NBC from 1974 to 1982. Church services in 1878 like the ones held in Walnut Grove Church, with Rev. Robert Alden as the pastor, may have appealed to crowds from yesteryear, but would seem grossly irrelevant today. Fast-forward to at least 1995. Our technological, fast-paced world is not impressed with anything that doesn't at least attempt to offer contemporary advancements. It's the difference between serving coffee or serving mochas! Today's youth are looking for connection and meaningful relationships. In days gone by, it was often about the buildings, furnishings, and ownership. I remember an elderly man who arrived at church to find a guest sitting in "his pew," aisle side. He immediately asked the man to find another seat as that was his spot. Sadly and understandably, the man left, never to return. And I could not blame him.

In another church, a young man walked into the building and did not remove his hat. A longtime member of the church in a harsh tone said to the boy, "Take off that hat or leave. You will not be disrespectful." Given that choice, the boy left, again never to return. And these were not isolated instances. Today's generation simply does not correlate hat-wearing with either respect or disrespect. They just like hats—both women and men!

Generational differences and viewpoints continue to make a lot of churches irrelevant and at times unfeeling and even harsh. How many have left churches because of rudeness and inflexibility on the part of generationally driven mind-sets? I'm afraid too many. Essentials and nonessentials must be continually weighed when it comes to generational mind-sets and teachings. Each generation holds to certain standards of conduct; however, when nonessentials become elevated above essentials, we run the risk of becoming offensive.

If you don't believe me, I challenge you to put a builder (born between 1927 and 1945), a boomer (1946–1964), a Generation X (1965–1976), a millennial or Gen Y (1977–1995), a Gen Z, I-GEN, or centennial (1996–TBD) in a room and ask them what church should look like. Johnny, bar the door. Run for your life! You will see what intense fellowship looks like. Things like tattoos, much-relaxed dress codes, instruments, LED boards, fog machines, coffee shops, Bible apps, loud music, high-fives, online giving, and more all make up the contemporary church. Inflexible mind-sets can sit on the side and criticize, but know one thing: Many under thirty years old will be criticized out the door, never to return.

Churches who care about winning the lost and making disciples need to understand that methods are never the telltale expression of the local church. Changing with the times is not optional; it's mandatory. I'm not talking about sin issues here; I'm discussing preferences.

Today, in the United States, between 1 and 2 percent of the existing 380,000 churches close their doors annually. Exact figures are hard to determine because of inaccurate reporting, and the fact that statistical crossing over from mainline denominations and evangelical churches is probable. Some estimates run as high as six thousand to ten thousand annual closings, but Taylor Billings Russell, Research Specialist for the Center for Analytical, Research and Data (CARD) says that more reliable research indicates that between 3,800 and 7,600 is a more accurate figure. Greg Smith from "So What Faith" concurs with this figure. Smith, a follower of the Way of Jesus/blogger/pastor/researcher, has been actively involved in local communities of faith throughout his life. My question, regardless of exact figures, remains, "Why?"

I know the reasons are many and varied, but I personally believe that irrelevance is one of the biggest culprits to local church demise. Church leaders across denominational lines are notorious for being afraid of change. Comfort zones are difficult to break out of, and it's all too easy to "do church as usual." However, brave leaders understand the fear of change perhaps constitutes the local church's greatest enemy. Today's mind-set simply will not tolerate ineffectiveness and lifeless pursuits. They are looking for momentum without defining it! But they know it when they see it! Holding on to the past is unacceptable to them.

Recent history records the pulling down and destruction of historical statues, mostly in the South. While we may adamantly disagree with such riotous actions, we have to understand that the past as perceived by many youth is an enemy of their "todays." My thinking, however, coincides with Philosopher George Santayana (1863–1952) who said in 1905 that "if we don't remember the past, we are condemned to repeat it." I personally am very saddened by these turn of events in our nation. What can local churches learn from these tragic historical events? Let me mention three:

1. We need to instill in our youth that the past is a treasured memory, and they must interpret today's events in light of history's successes and mistakes.
2. Embracing our past does not mean we agree with everything that happened. It simply holds us to a higher standard! History—good or bad—is not our enemy, but our instructor.
3. God is a "now" God. "*Now faith* is the substance" (Heb. 11:1). Spiritually speaking, tradition is where God was, not where God is. I'm referring here only to traditions that lead to outdated methods. Some traditions are priceless. Please don't mistake the two. If you don't believe me, try removing Christmas from the calendar and watch as both builders and centennials stage an uprising!

May God help us be like the tribe of Issachar recorded in 1 Chronicles 12:32a, "Of the men of Issachar, *men who understood the times*, with knowledge of what Israel should do." May he help us keep up with the times while always holding to his timeless message.

Questions to Ponder

1. Who determines essentials and nonessentials?

2. "Tradition is where God was, not where he is." What are your thoughts?

3. What can local churches learn from history?

4. Pastor, what are you doing to ensure the perpetuity of your local church?

26

Noah Got Drunk

*O*ver the past several decades, we have seen a decline in people having and showing respect for those in authority. Hate for authority equals rebellion. In Genesis 9, we read a story that demonstrates how God views authority and the premium he places on parental respect. I want to skim only the surface of this passage.

> Then Noah began farming and planted a vineyard. He drank of the wine and became drunk, and uncovered himself inside his tent. Ham, the father of Canaan, saw the nakedness of his father, and told his two brothers outside. But Shem and Japheth took a garment and laid it upon both their shoulders, and walked backward and covered the nakedness of their father; and their faces were turned away, so that they did not see their father's nakedness. When Noah awoke from his wine, he knew what his youngest son had done to him. So he said, "Cursed be Canaan; a servant of servants he shall be to his brothers." (verses 20–25)

To be sure, what Noah did was wrong. He got drunk! However, his actions did not excuse Ham's disrespect. This pride-filled son displayed an unruly heart. The other sons did what was right. They covered their father's nakedness and kept it quiet. Their respect for their dad overrode his temporary setback. Noah, who, I'm sure, regretted his poor example, also understood the absolute necessity of children honoring their parents, even when wrong, and pronounced a curse over Ham.

What's the overriding principle here? If we cannot respect the man or woman, at least respect the position they hold. Noah was still Ham's dad in spite of his behavior. I'm so thankful I was taught to respect my parents, teachers, police officers, adults, pastors, and other ministers of the Gospel, the flag, servicemen, presidents, and people in general.

I'll never forget the time I flew from Springfield, Missouri, to Cleveland, Ohio. After most everyone had boarded in Springfield, a large number of servicemen from nearby Fort Leonard Wood entered the aircraft. Suddenly, everyone in the plane jumped to their feet and began cheering and applauding our military personnel. It was an emotionally charged few minutes, and even some of the soldiers began weeping. It made me proud to be an American, and the respect shown that day brought tears of joy to all present. Showing respect makes people come alive in a way that nothing else can. It has to be taught and caught!

Did you watch the 2020 presidential debates? I was saddened and shocked by the blatant disrespect both opponents displayed. Name-calling, harsh tones, bullying, and overall rudeness characterized these political fiascos. I'm concerned about the unspoken trickling down effect these debates will have on our children and grandchildren. Oh, please, can we reverse this trend? Republican or Democrat, black or white, educated or uneducated, rich or poor, can we again learn to respect one another? We don't have to agree with others, but we do need to honor their personhood.

I've seen an attitude of disrespect in the local church as well. Some children grow up in homes that regularly serve "pastor casserole" for Sunday lunch. Insensitive, critical remarks about Sunday service represents the norm. The pastor's message is cruelly dissected, and pastoral performance called into question. Critical remarks about others in the church are also rehearsed. Some kids grow up hearing nothing but negative, unkind remarks about their pastor and/or their church. Is it any wonder they choose to leave the church after high school? Their souls become irreversibly wounded and a deep distrust and even animosity toward spiritual authority fills their hearts. Enough said. I pray that parents who engage in such spiritual murder repent and beg their probably now grown children to reconsider the church's grand role in the scheme of life and eternity.

Questions to Ponder

1. Is there anyone in my life I have openly disrespected?

2. Hate for authority equals rebellion. Am I holding on to rebellion at any level?

3. Read Genesis 9:20–25 again. What else do you derive from this story in terms of showing respect?

27

Emotional Residue

*I*ndividuals who experience trauma often quit developing emotionally at the point of their traumatic event. For example, if a young girl is sexually molested, she may quit developing emotionally at that time because to press past the trauma is too painful. That's why we deal with thirty-year-old twelve-year-olds. Do you understand? Clinical psychologist, Dr. Claudia Herbert from the Center for Trauma Healing and Growth at the Oxford Development Centre says,

> Too often when people have lived through a traumatic experience, their sense of the past and vision of the future stops—all that they can see in front of them are continuing pictures of the trauma that has befallen them. They begin to think and speak in extremes such as, "I'll always feel like this." "I never get over this." Or "I'm permanently damaged."

Emotional and mental pain can translate into the inability of people to become spiritually mature as well. A wounded soul finds it difficult to trust anyone after a traumatic experience. Many even have trouble trusting the Lord. They ask, "Why did He allow this to happen to me?" (See chapter 9.) And typically they read into everything! Even when it's not there to read into!

Those with father and mother wounds also bring their emotional residue into local churches. Counseling psychologist, Dr. Mari Kovanen, defines the father wound as "father absenteeism, whether emotionally or both emotionally and physically, and/or your father being very critical, negative and even abusive." She describes mother wounds this way: "The mother wound is your mother not being emotionally attuned and available to you as a child. She may have been present physically, but emotionally absent."

Sadly, many who are wounded in their family of origin, have difficulty getting along with their "brothers and sisters" in Christ. They tend to filter everything that happens or discussed through their pain. They desperately need soul healing. This, of course, is the church's secondary mission. I love what the late Dr. Richard Dobbins asked, "How much of the saved person will be saved?" You know this, but saved people don't always walk out their faith in a way pleasing to the Lord. I'm not talking about hypocrisy; I'm referring to the grip our wounded soul—mind, will, and emotions—has on us. Again, church families share a lot of similar characteristics of blood families. The emotional residue of our broken "yesterday's" works to bring further chaos and pain into our "today's." This is where intentionality to get along with others must remain the believer's goal. We must become quick forgivers.

Offenses are common, and the refusal to forgive one another drives people away from local churches. Unless individuals get honest with themselves and become willing to take responsibility for their anger and move past their pain, kingdom casualties result. To compound these issues, it is not uncommon for individuals to expect the pastor to take sides. Wise pastors insist that such fallout be corrected by applying the principles of Matthew 18:15–17.

> If your brother sins, go and show him his fault in private; if he listens to you, you have won your brother. But if he does not listen to you, take one or two more with you, so that *by the mouth of two or three witnesses every fact may be confirmed.* If he refuses to listen to them, tell it

> to the church (elders); and if he refuses to listen
> even to the church, let him be to you as a Gentile,
> and a tax collector.

All of us are broken and have unhealthy filters; however, by the same token, we all need to be responsible for our actions and attitudes. Conflict equals two, and when believers give and receive offenses, the local church suffers loss. The world needs to see how the church plays "show and tell." A viable witness for the Lord includes our willingness to not be emotionally driven, but spiritually driven when it comes to our relationships. Emotional instability places our testimony in jeopardy, which usually cannot be helped, but on the other hand, those with emotional issues cannot be given free expression. Bringing our wounds to the Lord for his healing touch validates our claims that the Gospel changes lives.

God, of course, is able to heal the oppressed and those who have been emotionally wounded. The sanctifying work of the Holy Spirit can be instantaneous, but in my pastoral experience, it is usually progressive. That's why wounded individuals need to be held back from leadership that puts them in the mainstream of church endeavor. Working with others usually spells trouble and dissension. As previously stated, hurt people tend to hurt people. Of course, these individuals are precious to God, but wisdom mandates their healing taking precedence over their having a ministry. Ministry opportunities that keep them away from interaction with others avoids possible setbacks in their healing process. Not always, but often, I see individuals who possess victim mentalities, or who fail to own their issues, or who display an unteachable spirit. Individuals who live in denial regarding traumatic issues and who refuse to embrace the healing process often struggle to find acceptance in local churches.

It is this pastor's opinion that emotionally wounded individuals need specialized one-on-one attention rather than a place of ministry. We should not risk placing these precious ones in the mainstream of ministry, as it might add to their already over-wrought emotions. If we do, they may implode and leave, never to return.

Questions to Ponder

1. Do you struggle with consistent runaway emotions? How do you keep them in check?

2. Think about the phrase "Hurt people hurt people." What comes to mind when you think about this truth?

3. "How much of the saved person will be saved?" How does Dr. Richard Dobbins's quote speak to you?

4. Why does the author recommend pastors not placing emotionally volatile individuals in key leadership positions?

28

A Higher Standard

To be fair, I had to include this reason why some people leave local churches. There are exceptional times when, because of corrupt, immoral, or unreasonable leadership—pastors, board members— individuals have no choice but to depart. Thank God, these times are far and few in between, but I have heard about legitimate decisions to leave. I'm not talking about "The preacher made me mad," or "The pastor did not visit my Aunt Susie," or "The pastor isn't feeding me." I'm talking about matters of conscience, the ongoing teaching of false doctrine, immorality, financial indiscretions, lying, sowing discord, or unrepentant communal sin in general. You see, pastors must be held to a higher standard than the people they lead. This may seem unfair, but I have always counted it an honor. With this being said, blessed are those who understand that pastors, too, are human and come equipped with their own set of faults and soul wounds.

I personally do not feel enough attention—teaching and encouragement—is given to heal the soul wounds of pastors. Mental health professor, Eduardo Duran, defines soul wounds in this manner: "Soul wounds relate to historical and intergenerational trauma. This trauma involves the recognition that horrifically violent experiences inflicted upon individuals in the past result in unhealthy outcomes that are passed on to one's offspring." Soul wounds are "broken places" deep within the recesses of the hearts (mind) that have not been exposed in a healthy manner and remain unhealed. Soul wounds, of course, affect the mind, will, and emotions. They explain the existence of post-conversion issues. Pastors also experience wounds in their family of origin, and most certainly as they navigate church ministry. Wounds that lead to unresolved anger, lust, insecurity, lying, depression, personality issues, unyielding control, alcoholism, and much more tend to infiltrate the hearts of many gifted and promising church leaders.

Pastors seldom have a safe place to download these deeply rooted issues. Sadly, many have met with betrayal when they trusted members of their congregation or even other pastors. Pastor friend, be careful who you tell what. Wisdom mandates that we seek solutions and deliverance, but in the right place. God has raised up Spirit-filled professionals to listen, advise, teach, and pray for you. Please search them out! To begin, let me recommend Emerge Ministries in Akron, Ohio. How many wonderfully gifted pastors have suffered embarrassment, ministry loss, and personal setbacks due to soul wounds that were never confronted? Oh, may we move past the stigma associated with pastoral imperfections and realize that pastors, too, are human beings who struggle with all the faults and failures brought on by life's pain-filled experiences.

I remember the times I suffered in silence when dealing with difficult people in ministry. Those times when my character flaws became apparent, or when I fell short of wise leadership. I know because it was my own untreated soul wounds that brought much harm to my third church. In the middle of one of the greatest revivals I've ever pastored, I fell apart. I was serving a country church that saw over seventy people come to Christ between January and March 1998. Holy excitement was off the charts! But I was a mess. A handful of people in the church became judgmental and accusatory toward me for reasons I still don't know. They were mean-spirited and unreasonable. And I became angry.

Regretfully, I used the pulpit to vent my anger toward individuals and issues in the church. Week after week, I lashed out, broadstroke fashion, aiming my misdirected anger toward the whole to get to a small faction. Over time, I noticed the people were becoming squeamish, and I justified it by saying, "Some folks simply hate spiritual authority and refuse to accept the uncompromised preaching of God's Word." Misdirected actions are sometimes smokescreens to hide hurt feelings, harbored resentment, and self-righteous zeal. Just recalling my delinquency makes me cringe!

Then people began leaving, and I became so very discouraged. After all, I was suffering for righteousness's sake. Or was I? One day, the Lord challenged my pulpit etiquette by speaking to me from Ephesians 6:4. "Fathers, do not exasperate your children." The Lord showed me that I was provoking people to anger through my preaching. No amount of justification could satisfy the conviction I felt. I had tried in vain to confront individuals and issues through preaching. My friend, these types of church strongholds do not come down by preaching; they come down only through prayer and righteous intervention behind the scenes. Paul's admonition in 2 Corinthians 10:1, 3–4, and 8 helped me put my preaching on a better course.

> By the meekness and gentleness of Christ, I appeal to you… For though we live in the world, we do not wage war as the world does. The weapons we fight with are not the weapons of the world. On the contrary, they have divine power to demolish strongholds… For even if I boast somewhat freely about the authority the Lord gave us for building you up rather than pulling you down, I will not be ashamed of it.

Continued assaults from the pulpit scattered the sheep. I abused the authority that came with the office of pastor. Wrong thinking attached itself to my thought processes. I preached to the minority at the expense of the majority. Still today, I grieve over the little ones that got caught in the cross fires of provocation. I'm so glad that God is faithful to restore, even when misguided zeal overrides godly wisdom. Take it from a pastor who learned the hard way. I was called to be a shepherd, not a sheep dog. Successful preaching encompasses not only what we say, but who we are. God's people need to understand that they reproduce who they are! However, because words are forces, they can bring healing or hurt.

I told myself it was righteous anger, but really, I was being a coward, not willing to privately deal with people. I was, in truth, crying out for those closest to me to help and protect me. However, some became insensitive and neglectful. Others took on an attack mode instead of lovingly confronting me. Sure, even loving feedback would have been tough to hear, but in retrospect, I believe my ministry in every church would have been more effective and perhaps even longer and healthier. Oh, how I could have used a "Barnabas" to encourage me during those times. Sometimes I feel that those who lead alongside pastors feel it their responsibility—almost job description—to keep the pastor in line.

Calling all those who work closely with pastors! Do everything in your power to make him or her the best pastor ever. Always remember to keep the bigger picture in focus. The success of your leader, your church, and community are at stake. Unfortunately, pastors many times short-circuit their effectiveness and potential to succeed. How I weep over these leaders who could have been so much more!

Throughout Scripture, we read about those who because of questionable character issues disqualified themselves from effective leadership. I again think of Samson whose leadership in Israel was cut short because of his moral indiscretions (iniquities). Pastors and other leaders who fall into sin and who embrace ongoing sinful patterns must be restored back to health and integrity. In some instances, they must step down temporarily. This is God's plan.

When in extreme cases, leaders refuse to repent and continue in their sinful ways, local churches are called upon to exercise tough love. Leaders, by virtue of their calling, are held to higher standards. But again, the goal of any failure is restoration. I know several pastors who effectively lead churches today who, at some time in their ministry, fell morally. They are surely trophies of divine grace. It's so important that local churches keep their eyes, not on the man of God, but on the Lord himself. Yes, honor him. Love him. Stand with him. And please, pray for him, asking the Lord to keep him strong in the day of battle and temptation. And also while praying, ask God to remind him that any successes he enjoys belong to the Lord!

Questions to Ponder

1. What improper leadership scenarios qualify as matters of conscience?

2. Why should leaders step down after moral failures?

3. Some in churches may feel it their duty to keep the pastor in line. How is this counterproductive?

4. What is a soul wound? What are some of the residual effects of those gone unhealed?

5. What are some of the ways individuals medicate their untreated soul wounds?

29

Trust Your Leader

$\mathscr{I}$ have given my life to the local church, and for that, I'm thankful. Overall, the journey has been wonderful. The good has far outweighed the bad. Most of the people I've served have been easy to work alongside. They have loved me and expressed appreciation in spite of my imperfections! However, there have been a few exceptions that took me to the edge of my good graces! Some people were difficult to lead because of their unwillingness to submit without becoming disagreeable.

Let me ask, have you ever been disappointed with a church leader? Of course you have! All of us meet with and probably cause disappointment at some level. I'm just sure that I've been the cause of somebody's anger! God calls us to learn and mature through those times.

In the scheme of any church's life, pastors have to sometimes make decisions that are misunderstood. During such times, choosing to trust the pastor is paramount. He often knows things that must be held in strict confidence. For example, during one Sunday service, a lady who was in an abusive relationship stood up during praise and worship and began yelling out the Ten Commandments in loud, rapid succession. Her interruption, of course, unnerved the entire congregation. Her voice tone was anger-filled and harsh. I immediately asked her to refrain from speaking because she was obviously out of order. When she refused to comply, ignoring my second request and becoming even louder, I finally asked the usher to remove her from the service. Later, her sordid story went public. Her alcoholic husband was maritally raping her! Her episode was a desperate cry for help.

That week two families left the church, charging that I was out of line. They used Scriptures from 1 Corinthians 12–14 to defend the woman's right to speak in such a way. They forgot the apostle Paul's admonition to conduct things "decently and in order" during public worship services. As the service leader, I was within my rights to stop the interruption. During such times, it behooves those in the service to trust the leadership of the pastor, understanding that he or she must give an account, not them! I've also had to deny individuals permission to do certain things, having confidential reasons for my decision. Pastoral prerogative may cause anger and feelings of not being appreciated. Let's face it. None of us see the broader picture in any given situation. As Dr. Richard Dobbins taught, "We view the parade through a hole in the fence!"

I have personally dealt with individuals who felt their gifts and callings were not being fully utilized in the church and who became disillusioned with me personally. They were unwilling to trust my insights and realize that I was holding privileged, confidential information. To discuss these matters would constitute gossip on my part. My parents made decisions when I was growing up that disappointed and angered me. In retrospect, they knew things I didn't, and it was their willingness to be misunderstood that protected me! And that's how pastoral leadership works.

Some leave a local church when they don't understand pastoral decisions and become unwilling to give leadership the benefit of the doubt. Partial insight may lead to inaccurate speculations, which can lead to hard feelings and even strife. Disappointments not tempered by the Holy Spirit can cause us to question leadership credibility and spawn rebellion.

Dr. Harry Yates and his wife Joanne Cash Yates have pastored Nashville's Cowboy Church for over thirty years. This prince of preachers and my friend told me many years ago, "There are two basic rules for every church: (1) The pastor is always right, and (2) when the pastor is wrong, see rule number one!" Of course, we both laughed, but behind the kidding is a subtle truth: God honors churches who honor their pastor. The best way to deal with pastoral malfeasance is to offer up consecrated prayer with a pure heart. God loves the local church, and initially the best way to correct any kind of misunderstanding or disagreement, one which gives the devil a black eye, is to place any concerns in the hands of the Lord. "The effectual fervent prayer of righteous people avails much" (James 5:16). Can I tell you? God will respond! He places a high premium on righteous pastoral conduct. This is one reason you need to keep your pastor at the top of your prayer list!

Many years ago, while sitting in a Sunday school class that delved into controversial issues, I began to sense growing dissension among strong personalities. I relayed my concerns during one class, and the end result caused a tidal wave of emotion. Admittedly in retrospect, I lacked wisdom in how I approached it but nonetheless felt that my concerns were legitimate. Like others in the class, I raised my hand to comment on a question at hand, and what happened next proved that my position in that house was one of a "hired hand," not as a respected leader.

Feelings got hurt, and during the ensuing weeks, many in the church became embroiled in a pastor versus other leaders' conflict. As the pastor, I felt it both right and prudent to maintain my stand. Members of the class were stirring controversy within the church, and as the watchman on the wall, I felt I had no choice but to recommend a different curriculum. One or two key individuals did not agree with my stand and subsequently incited a silent ground swell in the church. It was my considered opinion the enemy was using the subject matter to stir anger and a divisive spirit.

I, too, became angry, but for a different reason. It upset me that influential leaders challenged my ability and right to make such a decision. They wanted a townhouse meeting and a vote to determine the validity of my decision. I already had proven leadership in that particular church and felt betrayed. I wished others had given me the benefit of the doubt, but instead, the dissenters kept sowing discord until finally I was compelled to resign as pastor. I felt then, and still do, that the enemy scored a victory in that house. Later, my successor skillfully navigated and redirected the rebellion.

Pastor friend, there are times when you have to make decisions to protect the whole church, all the while taking the risk of being misunderstood. Pastoral decisions at times cause individuals to lash out unreasonably and without considering the negative impact it may have on the church. When tension surfaces, pastors must act accordingly. Such actions tie in with God's ongoing passion to win the lost. God is always looking for ways to draw people into the kingdom. Be careful. People need to understand that uninvited, even undesired change may be God's invitation to a renewed celebration of his grace in their life and the life of their church. Inflexibility and noncompliance may be the cause of a ministry not moving forward like it needs to. And none of us want that! Never be a hindrance, but always be helpful. If the pastor is wrong, God has a way of redirecting him. Such times make necessary the power of intensified prayer!

I knew a woman who beautifully operated in the gifts of the Holy Spirit for many years, but over time, she became self-righteous and even used the gifts to bring confusion instead of blessing to the church. Her pastor, she felt, began to emphasize the fruit of the Spirit over the gifts of the Spirit, and she became critical and divisive. The pastor explained that he was not against the gifts, but the infant church primarily needed to mature, and that the wrong emphasis on power gifts was bringing self-righteous, super-spiritual attitudes to the surface. She needed to trust the pastor's leadership instead of demanding her way, which by the way, showcased her carnality and obviously her underlying brokenness.

It's about what's best for his ongoing work of redemption in the lives of people who desperately need the Lord. Those who have been in the faith and in the church for years would do well to remember that the work of the Lord moves forward only through unity. Pastors are God's spokesmen and his conduit through which to flow. If you feel the pastor is misadvised, then pray for him. Don't criticize. The Lord is able to redirect and solidify the issue at hand. The pastor's reluctance to embrace issues, pet doctrines, and the implementation of certain practices, could be divinely driven. During those times, trust his leadership, knowing that God first speaks to and then through his leaders.

I have been victimized by individuals who felt that God spoke to them "to tell the pastor." This smacks of arrogance and division. This is a subversive attitude. Decisions that others disagree with are not the end of the world, but they could lead to the hindrance of God's work in a given church, at a given time, for kingdom purposes. Never allow what you want or what you think to override God's intended purposes. Again, it's not about you. It's about his work.

Questions to Ponder

1. Why is it important that we trust our pastors and other leaders?

2. A pastor once said, "At times churches play according to two separate and conflicting rules when it comes to discussing church issues. If pastors talk, they're gossiping. If others talk, they are expressing concern." What do you think?

3. How do we respond during those times when a pastoral decision leaves us in disagreement?

30

The Heart of Worship

Christian artist Matt Redman reminded us in his wonderful song, "Heart of Worship," that worship is all about Jesus.

When those who stand before us with instruments in hand and voices raised, really understand the true heart of worship, local churches weekly experience a touch from heaven. Worship that delights the heart of God and rids itself of performance-driven, image-conscious leaders, impacts individuals, churches, and entire communities. And the devil, heaven's original worship leader, understands this dynamic. That's why he works tirelessly to create division, offenses, and rifts on church stages. One area of high turnover in church life is that of worship leaders. Sadly, competitive and jealous attitudes often rise up in this area of church life. And everyone loses! Oh, may those who lead us dethrone themselves and enthrone Jesus!

In our circles, we used to call the worship segment the "song service." This usually meant singing random hymns and choruses, and sometimes taking requests from the floor! Over the past fifty years, we have seen a more calculated approach to worship. Most churches refer to it as "praise and worship." Why? Because any given worship time involves these two very unique aspects: praise and worship! What is praise? Ascribing honor and worth to our King, our Savior. We praise him for his glorious attributes, power, goodness, forgiveness, and his unending love as "psalms, hymns and spiritual songs" (Eph. 5:19) are lifted to the throne. The Bible tells us that "praise is comely to the believer" (Ps. 33:1). What does this mean? Praise literally dresses or adorns the believer. Christ followers, who love to praise, are some of the "best-dressed" people on the planet!

Not always, but usually, more upbeat songs are introduced as united voices blend together with clapping, hands extended, dancing, and other exuberant acts of worship—all directed heavenward. Few things match the beauty of praise as it flows out of the abundance of grateful hearts.

Then, we move into worship. While praise extols the goodness of the Lord, worship brings heaven to earth! We say it often: "God lives in the praises of his people" (Ps. 22:3). Heaven kisses the earth when a group of people come together in unity to give praise to God. And hearts tuned into God know it when there's a shift in the heavens!

The power of praise lifts "hands that hang down low" (Heb. 12:12). Praise ignites the heart with faith to believe God for the needs of our life. Praise "goes up," and worship brings the kingdom "down" to earth. "Let Your kingdom come and let Your will be done on earth as it is in heaven" (Matt. 6:10). I've seen people healed during worship. I've watched heavy hearts find peace and assurance under the weight of God's glory and witnessed the joy of the Lord as it washed over their faces. In the presence of God, emotions are stirred. Tears flow and hearts are made ready to receive the Word of God.

I personally do not see how any church can expect to experience any type of worship without first giving people time to lift up the praises of God. People walk into church many times with heavy burdens and the emotional and mental residue of the week covering them like a heavy blanket. Through praise we are able to cast off the heaviness that life sometimes puts on us.

> The Spirit of the Lord is upon me, because the Lord has anointed me to bring good news to the afflicted; He has sent me to bind up the brokenhearted, to proclaim liberty to captives and freedom to prisoners; to proclaim the favorable year of the Lord and the day of vengeance

of our God; to comfort all who mourn, to grant those who mourn in Zion, giving them a garland instead of ashes, the oil of gladness instead of mourning, the mantle of praise instead of a spirit of fainting. (Isa. 61:1–3)

Does every church move from praise to worship every time they gather? Of course not. But yielded hearts should expect and be open to receive a "piece of heaven on earth."

While praise and worship leaders are charged with leading this all-important aspect of church endeavor, they must always remember that platform leadership is a privilege, not an ego builder. Here's where the enemy trips up many. Pride must die in the presence of the one who has saved us by his grace and called us to exercise our gifts. Skilled musicians may bring excellence to the platform, but if hearts are not yielded and broken in the moment, that church will have a performance but not a life-altering venue. By the same token, platform presentation may lack in musical and vocal skills, but if hearts are tendered before the Lord, people will still experience God in the moment! Worship leaders who shame people—even bring rebuke—find that walls go up between the platform and the pews. Music that has been prayed over and surrendered to the Lord finds a resting place as a united flow moves over the church. I find that as worship leaders dismiss ego and exalt the one who has made redeemed life possible, the church never faces division on the platform.

As you probably know, Lucifer (Satan) was the worship leader of heaven. The Bible describes his fall this way: "You were blameless in your ways from the day you were created, until unrighteousness was found in you... Your heart was lifted up because of your beauty; you corrupted your wisdom by reason of your splendor. I cast you to the ground" (Ezek. 28:15 and 17). Do you remember when the seventy who had been sent ahead in pairs by Jesus to survey the evangelistic landscape, "returned with joy, saying, 'Lord, even the demons are subject to us in Your name.' And He said to them, 'I was watching Satan fall from heaven like lightning'" (Luke 10:17–18). Pride precipitated that fall, and ever since, the enemy works overtime to download that same pride in the hearts of worship leaders and others who help lead churches in praise to God. A praising church is a powerful and victorious church. However, egos not surrendered to Jesus often bring division to churches.

To me, the greatest attribute any worship leader can possess is humility. Credit-crazy and affirmation-driven worship leaders need to sit out until their focus is clear. Their rally cry should be, "Sirs, we must see Jesus" (John 12:21).

This also applies to those running the sound board! I've watched as those on stage battled with those in the sound booth. The purposes of God for each service are thwarted when people refuse to submit to one another. Canadian communication theorist Marshall McLuhan is noted for saying, "The medium is the message." Accordingly, nothing minimizes worship experiences like a poorly run sound board or an antagonistic operator. The medium—sound—is surely the message when it comes to an anointed worship service. All involved need to tuck their expertise, preferences, and anger under the blood of Jesus. The enemy shows up to church, along with our carnal nature. We dare not give either an audience.

Some, while reading this, may perhaps think, "Singing hymns is the best way to usher in God's presence." Still others may enjoy songs from Elevation Worship, or Hillsong, or Bethel Music, or from any number of contemporary Christian outlets. Others prefer Southern Gospel, or choirs, or solos, or whatever. Because anointed music, regardless of the genre, tears down demonic strongholds, disengages works of the enemy and lifts the worshiper up in heavenly places, you can see why the devil works tirelessly to move believers into a competitive mode.

When I mention Dallas Holm or Bill and Gloria Gaither and their Homecoming Friends, The Imperials, Sandi Patty, Carman, Andrae Crouch, or other Christian artists time relevant to me, many of my younger pastor friends say, "Who?" These artists and more were the ones in the Christian spotlight back in the 1970s when I was a new believer. I still love their music. My friend, can we stop comparing notes, as it were, and just worship? Whatever carries you into the presence of God is not the only right genre; it's what works for you! Let me encourage you to put aside your favorites and under-stand that heaven will be a worshipping place and earth is our dress rehearsal.

Do you know who the primary worship leader is in your church? It's your pastor! He's the one who seeks God for the direction your church should go. He's responsible for paving the way for true praise and worship to happen in your church. Wise pastors are strategical-ly-driven—not controlling—but they understand that the anointed preaching of God's Word is made easier by anointed worship! Any worship leader will tell you that their preparation to lead is birthed during specially scheduled rehearsals so that when they stand to lead, the anointing on them spills into the room. At that time, it's defi-nitely not about them, but they become conduits for the Holy Spirit to flow. Worship leaders who become upset when those they lead don't respond in an expected fashion, need to understand that wor-ship is both an event and a process. Effective, Holy Spirit-led worship leaders must remain in touch with the house. Their eyes need to be focused on crowd participation, not constantly closed in private wor-ship. Their privilege is to lead, not to get caught up in their preferred style and ignore their audience. I've seen worship leaders who played music but did not lead people. In short, they presented concerts instead of worship experiences. Worship that does not initiate crowd participation causes many to withdraw in disappointment. They eas-ily become disengaged when song selections best used for private worship become the norm. Remember, there are many good worship songs that were written for personal expression but not for corpo-rate gatherings. Leaders who do not understand the "flow" aspect of worship reduce set lists to a choppy expression of songs that neither connect nor entice people to enter into worship. When people gaze around the room, talk, or appear disengaged during worship services, something is wrong. And when church is over, remind the people that the greatest way to worship the Lord is by the way we live. We worship him through our lifestyle!

Questions to Ponder

1. Who is the "heart of worship"?

2. Did you know that Lucifer was at one time heaven's worship leader? Read Isaiah 14 and Ezekiel 28 to glean more details.

3. What is the difference between praise and worship?

4. Did you know that your pastor is the real worship leader in your church? Explain.

5. Why is humility a mandatory part of the worship leader's life?

31

Moved, but Not Changed

Wherefore Saul sent messengers unto Jesse, and said, "Send me David my son, who is with the sheep." And Jesse took a donkey laden with bread, and a bottle of wine, and a goat, and sent them by David his son to Saul. And David came to Saul, and stood before him; and he loved him greatly, and he became his armor bearer. And Saul sent to Jesse, saying, "Let David, I pray you, stand before me; for he has found favor in my sight." And it came to pass, when the evil spirit from God was upon Saul, that David took a harp, and played with his hand; so Saul was refreshed, and was well, and the evil spirit departed from him. (2 Sam. 16:19–23)

*A*fter the Lord rejected Saul as king, his life took a quick downward spiral. He became a tormented man. The musical anointing on David was the one thing that could temporarily soothe Saul's mind. So whenever Saul became out of sorts, David's harp would settle him. His inner turmoil became subdued. But understand, *Saul was moved, but not changed.* Anointed music has a way of soothing the savage beast!

I have loved the hymns of the church since my boyhood. Humorously, I recall many of them were written either very high or very low. We either sang from the rooftop or in the basement! And I also remember how the hymns moved me emotionally. I cried in church, not because I was sad, but because the music stirred me. "How Great Thou Art" still takes me to an emotional high. "Pass Me Not" takes me back to the night when I gave my heart to Christ. This song of invitation became "the song of my salvation." The lyrics and music moved me to tears and catapulted me to the altar. Even today, I fight back tears when I hear this wonderful hymn. Bill and Gloria Gaither's Homecoming Friends sing it like none other!

Back then, we primarily sang *about* the Lord. Nowadays, it seems that a lot of church music sings *to* the Lord. Neither is right or wrong, and both styles draw emotional responses. Music carries us into the presence of the Lord and opens our hearts to receive the preached Word. A lot of church music is experiential in content. It tells a story that ignites an emotional response or at least strikes a heart string that brings tears. With this in mind, and as much as we Christians love such music, it stops short of solidifying our faith.

Jesus told the woman at the well, "They that worship God, must worship Him in spirit and in truth" (John 4:23). This verse is twofold in its intent. Jesus potentially was telling the woman that we need to worship in spirit (in song) and in truth (the preached Word). In other words, we need a balance of the two. As wonderful as worship music is, we cannot build a solid faith on just worship. We need the Word! One prepares the heart for the other! Who wants solely an unemotional faith? Not me! But by the same token, nor do I want a shallow faith.

Now, let me draw out a valid principle from the above story about David playing his harp for Saul. The king, by this time, was moving toward a reprobate condition. His heart was far from God, and he knew deep inside that he had forsaken his righteous heritage. Although he secretly despised David, he recognized the precious anointing on the psalmist's life. And he knew that with that anointing came peace—something that usually escaped him. David played his harp and Saul became temporarily calmed. Occasional bouts of peace were better than constant turmoil. You see, *Saul was moved, but not changed!* Genuine encounters with Jesus Christ not only move our emotions but change our lives.

A Christianity that does not transform behavior is not a biblical Christianity. On August 4, 1970, I experienced a life-changing, emotionally charged encounter with the Lord. I wept freely and deeply for two hours. I felt as if the weight of the world had been lifted from me. I felt clean from the inside out. When I got up from that altar, *I was not only moved, but changed.* I was born again. The Holy Spirit had set up housekeeping inside my spirit. I was "no longer dead in my trespasses and sins" (Col. 2:13).

Old habits and sins fell out of my life. No one had to tell me that cursing, premarital sex, adultery, lying, stealing, uncontrolled anger, getting drunk, etc., were no longer acceptable. The indwelling Spirit brought conviction. I wasn't perfect, but I was forgiven! Worship and the Word changed my life. Both were instrumental in bringing me to saving faith. Please understand. Your faith cannot ride on your emotions; your emotions must ride on your faith. All of us love the emotions that anointed, Christ-honoring music produces, but unless the Word is mixed with faith, it cannot produce long-term effects.

Our faith must run deeper than our emotions. The preached Word, mixed with faith, reveals sin and brings conviction (Heb. 4:2). Conviction, then, demands a verdict. Committed Christians allow their emotions to serve them, never master them. Those solid in faith understand that to be moved upon emotionally is quite all right, but God's desire is that we allow his Word to "transform us into the same image from glory to glory" (2 Cor. 3:18). The Word and the Spirit work in unity to bring about life change. God gives us emotions to help us along our journey. I appreciate it when the Spirit of the Lord invokes an emotional response inside me, but I appreciate it more knowing that his Word "is living and active and sharper than any two-edged sword, and piercing as far as the division of soul and spirit of both joints and marrow, and able to judge the thoughts and intentions of (my) heart" (Heb. 4:12).

Perhaps like you, I listen primarily to Gospel music. I love praise and worship. I enjoy the music of several Christian artists. I have memorized a lot of hymns and choruses from yesteryear and embrace most contemporary praise and worship. But I became determined not to "worship worship." My desire is to allow whatever style to draw me into his presence in such a way that it opens my heart to "receive the engrafted word, which (together) are able to save my soul" (James 1:21).

Where am I going with this? It has been my concerned observation that many today have left the local church for some of the reasons I have discussed in this book, only to feel that Christian music, in whatever form adequately replaces God's original intention—worship *and* the Word. I'm afraid that *many are moved but not changed.*

Questions to Ponder

1. What role do emotions play in the Christian life?

2. "A Christianity that does not transform behavior is not a biblical Christianity." What does this mean to you?

3. Is it possible to "worship worship?" How?

32

Church Hoppers

*W*hy do pastors encourage individuals not to bounce from church to church? To me, the answer is simple. The Scriptures discourage it! Psalm 92:13 says, "Those who are planted in the House of the Lord will flourish in the courts of God." What does it mean to be planted? It means to be faithful to one church. Why do healthy plants continue to grow? Because they're planted in one location and not uprooted. Christians who refuse to consistently attend the same faith community welcome instability into their walk. I've seen people bounce around like ping-pong balls, only to spend their lives in confusion. Ironically, they know enough of God's Word to be dangerous to the cause of Christ, themselves, and others!

Christians need to get into a holy groove. No one church has all the right answers, and while the Bible remains inerrant and infallible, we are not! However, when believers choose to play the field, they could end up not knowing the truth from a lie. The enemy loves to mix them up.

I know a man who in his twenties attended a different church almost every Sunday morning. Many of the churches were led by leaders who were brazen enough to say, "Our church is the only one that preaches it right." Sadly, he even attended churches that strayed from orthodox Christian teaching and in practice were classified as cults. I begged him to find a good Bible-believing, Bible-preaching church and stay put. But time and exposure to so many different and often diametrically opposing doctrines finally drove him to give up on church altogether. That was over forty years ago. Today he is bitter and a self-proclaimed enemy of the local church.

Those who prefer to church hop sometimes possess a rebellious core. They secretly despise spiritual authority and refuse to submit to ongoing balanced teaching that calls them into accountability for their ungodly attitudes, wrong conduct, and inconsistent character. Some refuse to receive correction, which is a sign of spiritual decay. Instead, they often bash churches, pastors, other leaders, and Christians in general, making it their habit to wander aimlessly. In my experience, some who refuse to attend one church end up spiritually compromised. Those who do not acknowledge basic core values centering around the person of Jesus Christ become prey to deceiving spirits. And unfortunately, there are churches that do not believe or teach the basic core values of our faith.

For the purposes of this book, I want to reintroduce two works that basically outline the nonnegotiable tenets of our faith. First, the Apostle's Creed: "I believe in God the Father, Almighty Creator of Heaven and earth; and in Jesus Christ, his only Son, our Lord, who was conceived by the Holy Spirit, born of the Virgin Mary, suffered under Pontius Pilate, was crucified, died and was buried."

Next, Paul beautifully summarizes the mystery of the Gospel in 1 Timothy 3:16. It is one of the most pivotal verses in the Bible: "And without controversy great is the mystery of godliness: God was manifested in the flesh, justified in the Spirit, seen by angels, preached among the Gentiles, believed on in the world, received up in glory."

Emotionally driven Christians often move from church to church, looking for the next great service, move of God, high-intensity preaching, signs, and wonders or emotional highs in general. This, too, is sad because God tends to move his people—individually and corporately—through seasons. We all go through highs and lows in our Christian life. Remaining planted in one local church brings balance and stability into the believer's life. I have never felt it right to undermine worship styles and orders of service, as I understand there are many streams of Christian endeavor. One preacher said, "There are many flavors!" People need to go where they are comfortable, as long as it is Christ-centered.

Historically, churches tend to emphasize one member of the Trinity in their appeal and vision. For example, churches that mostly speak of God tend to emphasize social concerns and become heavily involved in civic interests. Churches that emphasize Jesus are typically what evangelicals refer to as "soul-winning" churches. In other words, their service structure is soteriologically driven, always seeking to win the lost to Christ. Then, churches that primarily emphasize the Person and work of the Holy Spirit tend to be intensity-driven, placing much emphasis on the gifts of the Holy Spirit while offering emotionally charged services. Truthfully, all three should preach "Christ and Him crucified" (1 Cor. 2:2). None of these are wrong, and many churches are a combination of all three. My point is that we need all three to spread the Gospel. Let's bring balanced ministry into our churches!

I've observed that many people choose their church according to their personality type. This, in my opinion, is both good and bad. Good if it offers a place to serve and grow as a believer. Bad if it does not challenge individuals to deepen their faith and find a richer, life-changing experience with Jesus Christ. Usually, when I ask people if they are Christians, I hear, "I'm a Baptist," "I'm a Catholic," "I'm a Methodist," etc. Many believers define themselves by their church instead of their Savior!

Jesus's high priestly prayer recorded in John 17, is not about a one world Church, which we should all disdain, but rather that true believers put aside their labels, and together impact the world with the heart-transforming Gospel of Jesus Christ. Ask the Lord to give you an unconditional love for the many streams of Christian endeavor. There is power in unity. I don't necessarily agree with everything other churches teach, but as long as the basic tenets of the Christian faith are intact, I can walk in unity with other believers not of my persuasion.

All who preach Christ and him crucified, the Son of God, and the only way to God, are brethren. We are not competitors, but we commend one another to God's grace and favor. Those who randomly move from church to church remain unsettled and unfulfilled. Is it ever all right to attend a service of another Christ-honoring church? Of course, the potential reasons are too numerous to mention. The bottom line, however, is making those times the exception, not the rule.

Questions to Ponder

1. Read Psalm 92:13. What does it say to you personally?

2. Do you know what you believe doctrinally and why you believe it?

3. After reading this chapter, can you give three reasons why the author discourages church hopping?

33

Three Parables

$\mathcal{L}$uke 15 records three parables that center around the word *lost*. Verses 4–7 speak of the *lost* sheep. Verses 8–10 tell the story about a *lost* coin. Verses 11–32 relay the story of a *lost* son, commonly known as the prodigal son. The sheep was lost due to his own carelessness. The coin was lost due to the action of others. The son was lost due to his own behavior. I have often contemplated the true meaning of these parables. Some suggest that when individuals leave local churches, caring pastors should always go after them—regardless of the circumstances under which they left.

I used to struggle with the proper interpretation of these "earthly stories with a heavenly meaning," until I discovered that each parable self-interprets. In all three, Luke tells a story then explains it. The story of the lost sheep refers to *"one sinner."* The lost coin also tells us, "There is joy in the presence of the angels of God over *one sinner* who repents" (verse 10). Again, in the story of the prodigal, the emphasis is upon repentance: "I will go up and go to my father, and will say to him, 'Father, *I have sinned* against heaven, and in your sight'" (verse 18). These parables deal strictly with individuals who repent, who move from being lost to being found. *Luke refers to either new converts or those who repent after willfully falling into sin. He does not reference those who refuse to repent.* In retrospect of my churches, I spent a lot of time and energy pursuing "sheep, coins, and prodigal sons" who had no intention of making things right. In the end, they still left, many times after making me grovel and letting them mistreat me. We are mandated by Scripture to forgive others when they sin, whether due to their carelessness, or because of the actions of others, or because of their own sinful behavior. That's a given. We have to release them to the Lord. They are not "the enemy." However, when they make premeditated decisions, we must let them live with their choices.

In all three parables, personal decisions were made to sin— against God and others. And in all three cases, repentance was the key to restoration. The sheep, the woman, and the prodigal son were described as sinners who needed to repent, or to change their mind regarding their conduct. When individuals leave churches, their conduct must also be weighed in light of their parting attitude. Did they leave because they were careless? Did they leave because of others who influenced them? Did they leave because of willful, sinful conduct? No matter the reason, people are called to give an account.

Above all, pastors must protect the sheep, no matter how difficult. Precious lives hang in the balance. Face it. There comes a time when pastors must quit worrying about being "Mr. Nice Guy" and do what it takes to defend the flock. We are responsible for our own decisions and cannot blame others for our actions. In all three parables, sin is the culprit, and repentance is the solution. When individuals leave local churches, their conduct cannot be swept under the rug. All of us are called to live righteously in the family structure. None of us are islands unto ourselves. We cannot move through life unaccountable for our actions.

What about those who leave unannounced but were not problematic? I personally struggle with their irresponsibility and lack of courtesy. In other words, their conduct is inappropriate because of how they leave everyone hanging. They leave mysteriously, causing doubt and creating unnecessary suspicion. The enemy of the Church rides piggyback off these unfortunate exits. Those who remain many times believe the worst-case scenario, often borrowing trouble through negative speculation. When this happens, individuals need to give their pastor the benefit of the doubt, trusting his leadership integrity. I've had to forgive these individuals and place them in God's hands. They, too, must give an account. These individuals are not lost but are usually misguided. Some leave churches for careless reasons. Some leave because of the actions of others. And some leave because of rebellious hearts. Regardless of their reasons, all three parables in Luke 15 refer to sinners who need to repent.

God's ideal conduct for believers who are part of a local church family, who may experience fallout for any reason, is to make clear their intentions by humble means. This requires a coming together to clear up misunderstandings, explain any disagreements, and to genuinely offer best wishes and mutual love. In other words, people need to leave right, if they feel they must. From my perspective, leaving should be the exception, not the rule. God's people need to treat each other in such a way that unbelievers say, "My, how they love one another." John 13:35 says it all: "By this shall all men know you are My disciples, if you love one another." Remember, God's love is unconditional, not conditional. We love period, not "if."

Questions to Ponder

1. True or False: Pastors should always follow up on people who leave their church, no matter the reasons. Why or why not?

2. People who leave a church mysteriously create what kind of concerns?

3. The three parables in Luke 15 are stories that center on what one word? Please elaborate.

34

Peacemakers, Not Peacekeepers

*W*hat's another reason people potentially leave churches? This chapter specifically addresses a very important principle of pastoral leadership that, if taken seriously, might initially create an exodus, but over the long run produces a healthy, peace-filled church. I have come to understand that great churches are not built overnight. Isaiah 28:10 (*NLT*) reminds us: "He tells us everything over and over—one line at a time, one line at a time, a little here and a little there." Just as the Christian life is a marathon, not a sprint, local church pastors need to understand that event-driven churches may produce numbers, but not always health! Slow, steady foundational growth creates stronger churches in the long run. A church may experience exponential growth, but pray when that happens the spiritual foundation holds firmly. That's why Jesus stresses the need for peacemakers, not peacekeepers!

"Blessed are the peacemakers for they shall be called children of God" (Matt. 5:9). Jesus did not say, "Blessed are the peacekeepers," He said, *"Blessed are the peacemakers."* So what's the difference between peacekeepers and peacemakers? Plenty! Pastors, other leaders, and many in our churches have misunderstood the important difference. Churches and organizations in general often possess troubled individuals who remain potentially divisive and have to be constantly monitored by leaders who work feverishly to keep the peace. Really, what's needed are leaders who decisively and wisely act to bring about permanent solutions, thus ridding the church of ongoing root issues. The end result will be lasting peace and guaranteed perpetuity. In other words, it will be healthy!

In each of my churches, I was called to be a peacemaker. Peacemakers are never popular, but when righteous leadership confronts counterproductive believers who act in ungodly ways, the church is better off in the long run. After all, souls hang in the balance, and we dare not allow unruly hearts to thwart what God wants to do in a given situation. Literally, entire communities are at stake. I'd rather lead one hundred people living in peace than two hundred living in strife! Peacemakers confront in love and at times firmly, but when it's all said and done, God's house is worth fighting for!

That's why I go to great lengths to righteously shepherd Hope Community Church. Did you know that Christians can operate under demonic influence? Put a peacekeeper in the mix and the kingdom of God suffers defeat. In 2 Timothy 2:23–26, Paul writes to believers in conflict:

> Refuse foolish and ignorant speculations, knowing that they produce quarrels. The Lord's bondservant must not be quarrelsome, but be kind to all, able to teach, patient when wronged, with gentleness correcting those who are in opposition, if perhaps God may grant them repentance leading to the knowledge of the truth, and they may come to their senses and escape from the snare of the devil, having been held captive by *him* to do *his* will.

The pronouns "him" and "his" refer to the devil. Peacemakers move forward in boldness to confront such wrongdoing. When these types of issues go unchallenged, the enemy literally declares "open season" on the church or whatever group might be involved and wreaks havoc. Vision is destroyed and precious lives are short-changed.

These things must not be allowed to fester. You may say, "Pray about it, and God will take care of it." I say, "Yes, pray. Pray hard.

Then act!" Oliver Cromwell at the Battle of Edgehill in 1642 is supposed to have told his Roundhead troops in the opening fight of the English Civil War, "Put your trust in God, my boys, but mind to keep your powder dry." Righteous strategies prevail! I have seen churches struggle year after year because Christians have never been taught the necessity of having peacemakers in leadership instead of peacekeepers. And sadly, good people often leave rather than being caught up in drama and division.

Pastors who refuse to confront unrighteous issues shoot themselves in the foot. No one in his right mind enjoys confrontation, but I think it's because we have bought into a lie when it comes to peacemaking. Of course, we do not want to purposely hurt anyone's feelings, but here's the bottom line: It's not about hurt feelings when church unity is at stake; it's about bringing corrective and righteous order to situations that can potentially end up bringing widespread dissension. And naturally, these times should be handled through prayer and confidentially.

Why then does Jesus extol peacemaking over peacekeeping? Because peacemakers make possible the uninterrupted flow of God's Spirit while peacekeepers try to please everyone and never see real peace. This principle holds true for any group of people. Confusion reigns where an undercurrent of strife is allowed to remain. Loving confrontation is necessary.

The word *confrontation* conjures up negative feelings; however, to confront does not mean having to yell, scream, threaten, or overtake someone by force. Everyone deserves wise instruction and the right to express themselves in a quiet, nonthreatening manner. The necessity of peacemakers versus peacekeepers works in every office, school, family, business, organization, and church. The principles are still the same. Let me explain through definition.

What is a peacekeeper? Peacekeepers are fickle. They operate in fear and allow loud voices and controlling spirits to rule the roost. They are fearful and often reel under the weight of public opinion and high-intensity voices. They cave in to manipulative and threatening schemes. They try to appease instead of confronting the canker within. Peacekeepers hate confrontation. For them, to confront requires more than they're willing to lose. That's why angry people often go unchallenged—they work in the dark and behind the scenes, and peacekeepers seldom meet their nemesis head-on. Peacekeepers usually end up losing their integrity and self-respect. They become chameleons, championing who they're with at the time. They try their best to please everyone and to keep everyone happy. In the long run, they end up pleasing no one!

Peacekeepers often are aware of underlying currents of discord and upheaval where peace is crowded out and tension reigns. But fear keeps them from acting with boldness and self-assurance. They live in frustration until they move from "keeping" to "making." Sadly, spiritually discerned people are often held at bay because of the intimidating spirit they face. They often find themselves caught in the middle of battles where opposing minds are led by peacekeepers. When strong leaders take on troubled situations, those in their charge feel a sense of protection. Put a peacekeeper in leadership and you have a mess on your hands—a weak church, business, or organization. Chaos is apt to reign. Remember, Christians sometimes operate under demonic principles. Strong peacemakers are necessary to call them out.

Pastors who refuse to operate as peacemakers often end up losing their influence and subsequently their respected ability to lead a given church. How many resignations have resulted because of pastors who allowed fear to drive them, instead of boldly rising up and fighting the good fight? I can ask this question with a degree of authority as I literally had to leave two churches because of my refusal to become a peacemaker.

What is a peacemaker? Peacemakers deal with root issues. They expose the underlying problems. They get to the bottom of conflict. And they make decisions based on what's best for the whole instead of the one. They sometimes make unpopular decisions, all the while keeping their integrity and self-respect intact. In short, they are willing to be misunderstood. And many times they are. Accusations of playing favorites, being unfair, and harsh often surface. But peacemakers stand firm in their convictions and decisions—right or wrong!

Timothy, at the request of Paul, functioned as a peacemaker when two women in the church at Philippi became embroiled in a conflict that threatened the unity of the entire church. He writes, "I urge Euodia and I urge Synteche to live in harmony in the Lord… I ask you to help these women" (Phil. 4:2–3). The Scriptures provide no details, but you can be sure that two women were called to task and a potentially divisive situation was righteously resolved, as Paul fought diligently to keep his beloved church moving forward.

Naturally, there are some battles not worth fighting. However, when the health of your church, your home, your business, or whatever is threatened from the inside out, you need to rise up and become a peacemaker. If a pastor refuses to do what's best, the church may suffer permanent decline. Jesus emphatically tells us that peacemakers are recognized as "children of God." And heaven backs those who do the right thing, regardless of what others think.

Are you a leader? Remember, being a peacemaker may not always be popular, but it will bring health and stability into any group of people. In all probability, people will leave, but any fallout must be seen as a preventive measure that curtails even worse end results. And most important, the favor of God!

Questions to Ponder

1. What are some of the primary differences between a peacemaker and a peace-seeker?

2. Read 2 Timothy 2:23–26 again. What does this passage say about demonic principles that potentially operate in a Christian's life?

3. The word "confrontation" conjures up negative emotions. What approach can peacemakers take to diffuse potential stress-filled situations?

35

The Great Falling Away

We are living in the final days before the coming of the Lord. This I strongly believe. The rapture of the Church is imminent. One of the trademarks of the pre-rapture Church will be a great falling away from God's revealed truth. It stands to reason that not only will many leave the faith but also leave the local church. This is a sad but prophesied reality. I believe what Jesus predicted is upon us. In Matthew 24:12–13a, He describes the end times with these words: "And because lawlessness will abound, the love of many will grow cold. But he who endures to the end shall be saved." A spirit of lawlessness, or rebellion, is filling the earth today. In my sixty-five years, I have watched as this dreadful spirit has brought turmoil to nations, staged coups, and set the stage for the eventual revelation of the "man of lawlessness."

In recent months, riots, looting, and violence have filled the streets of our major cities. Sex trafficking, racism, rape, and murder have skyrocketed. Evening newscasts aired a never-before-seen sight on January 6, 2021, as a radicalized mob stormed our nation's capitol building. Many shouted hate-filled slogans, and tragically, some even used the name of Jesus to justify their actions. Did you know that Christians can be right in principle but wrong in conduct? Misguided prophetic voices filled Facebook posts and other venues, inciting otherwise godly people to respond in ways unbecoming for believers in Jesus. Local churches had to avert division and conflict due to a runaway presidential election. Whether Republicans or Democrats, it's time for all of us to weep over a divided nation.

"Let the priests, the Lord's ministers, weep between the porch and the altar, and let them say, 'Spare Your people, O Lord, and do not make Your inheritance a reproach, a byword among the nations.'" Why should they among the peoples say, 'Where is their God?'" (Joel 2:17).

Seemingly, in many sectors the Church has lost its salt. Culture has influenced many away from the house of God and the God of the house. Empty, dilapidated churches line our streets, both in cities and rural areas. Second Thessalonians 2:1–3 speaks of that day:

> Now brethren, concerning the coming of our Lord Jesus Christ and our gathering together to Him, we ask you, not to be soon shaken in mind or troubled, either by spirit or by word or by letter, as if from us, as though the day of Christ had come. Let no one deceive you by any means, for that Day will not come *unless the falling away comes first*, and the man of sin is revealed, the son of perdition, who opposes and exalts himself above all that is called God or that is worshiped, so that he sits as God in the temple of God, showing himself that he is God.

Surely, Jesus is coming soon!

Deception abounds on every hand. Deception comes when revealed truth is traded for a lie. Christ-honoring local churches are the gatekeepers of truth, and when individuals absent themselves from that truth, they open themselves up to lying spirits. Romans 2:23 says, "They exchange the truth of God for a lie." Eventually, God "gives people up" to a depraved mind and a hardened heart. Usually, their depravity leads to moral bankruptcy. Someone once said, "God doesn't give up on people, but he does give them over when they continue to reject his righteous judgments."

I have with great trepidation watched as many who once knew the goodness of the Lord now exhibit strong disdain toward the things of God. They no longer care about spiritual matters and fit into one or more of the following twenty descriptions the apostle Paul listed in 2 Timothy 3:1–2.

> In *the last days* perilous times will come: For men will be lovers of themselves, lovers of money, boasters, proud, blasphemers, disobedient to parents, unthankful, unholy, unloving, unforgiving, slanderers, without self-control, brutal, despisers of good, traitors, headstrong, haughty, lovers of pleasure, rather than lovers of God, having a form of godliness, but denying its power.

I read these descriptions, and I want to cry. These dynamics are unfolding before our very eyes. The trickle-down effect will surely see people leaving the local church. This, I feel to be a true and tried correlation. I beg you. Stay firmly planted in the house of God!

Questions to Ponder

1. What is the correlation between "the falling away" and lawlessness?

2. "Having a form of godliness" refers to what?

3. One of the twenty characteristics mentioned in 2 Timothy 3:1–2 says, "Lovers of pleasure, rather than lovers of God." Can you elaborate?

36

Comparisons

$\mathcal{H}$ave you ever compared yourself with someone else? Did you come up short? Did you draw the short straw? We usually do when we play the comparison game. I, too, have fallen prey to this terrible temptation. Other pastors always had larger congregations and budgets, nicer facilities, larger salaries, better cars, vacations, and benefits; and to be sure, they were better preachers than I. However, in the scheme of eternity God only created one me! And one you! And he calls us "good"! "And God saw everything he had made, and behold, it was very good" (Gen. 1:31). For that reason, we need not compare ourselves to others. Jesus is our measuring point. Frankly, to compare ourselves to others is to insult the wisdom of God.

You are uniquely created by God to make a difference in your generation and to come alongside the rest of God's "designs" to corporately impact your world with the Gospel of Jesus Christ. Everyone plays a significant role! I have gifts you may not have and vice versa. We are not called to compare but to complement one another. We learn from one another and draw strength from our differences! I love what Dr. Richard Dobbins said about this concept as it pertains to married couples. He said, "If you're both exactly the same, one of you is not necessary!" But everyone matters. You matter! And we need one another. So when we compare ourselves to others, we waste precious time and short-circuit our potential. We may tire of feeling inadequate and never good enough. But we do it to ourselves.

Even the great apostle Paul struggled with comparing himself to others. This is what he came to believe:

> For we dare not make ourselves of the number or compare ourselves with some that commend themselves; but they, measuring themselves by themselves, and comparing themselves among themselves, are not wise. But we will not boast of things without our measure, but according to the measure of the rule which God has distributed to us, a measure to reach even unto you. (2 Cor. 10:12–13 KJV)

Did you fully understand what Paul is saying here? Neither did I, so let's read this passage from another translation:

> We do not dare to classify or compare ourselves with some who commend themselves. When they measure themselves by themselves and compare themselves with themselves, they are not wise. We, however, will not boast beyond proper limits, but will confine our boasting to the sphere of service God himself has assigned to us, a sphere that also includes you. (NIV)

What was Paul saying? Let's outline it:

1. We should not compare ourselves to others.
2. We need not think more highly or less of ourselves than others.
3. We should be content with the assignment God has given us.
4. We should appreciate one another's differences.

Now, let's discuss comparisons as they pertain to individuals leaving local churches. God has either called you to a specific local church, or he hasn't. I say this with 100 percent conviction. Often I have wondered what it would be like to spend my life with one body of believers. I have several pastor friends who have successfully led their church for thirty-plus years. Obviously, my assignments have made long tenures impossible (or so I thought). My calling, for the most part, has been to help troubled churches heal after experiencing internal turmoil. Admittedly, I have often wondered what I've missed by continually moving from church to church. Like I stated earlier, the culprit was discontentment. However, overall I have enjoyed my journey! So what are some of the benefits to staying in the same church? Here's a few:

1. You get to grow with those of similar faith.
2. You get to establish ongoing relationships that last a lifetime.
3. You get to establish solid, ongoing relationships that guide, protect, and bless your life.
4. You get to experience the joy of "pressing toward the mark" together.
5. You get to share in one another's joys, sorrows, and everything in between.

So how does comparing often cause people to leave churches? In today's consumer-driven culture, many in local churches are tempted to compare pastoral personalities, preaching styles, worship music, facilities, length of services, age of congregation, chairs versus pews, availability of small groups, attendance, doctrinal issues, kids and youth ministries, and even nonessential issues. I understand some of this "shopping" to a point, but I also believe in a higher principle that I feel should determine where we attend church: *Where does the Lord want us?*

To me, this overrides personal preference if and when we realize that all churches have to start somewhere. One of the most unreasonable, even cruelest things individuals can do is constantly compare their pastor to former pastors. Paul had to set the Church at Corinth straight in this regard. In 1 Corinthians 1:11–17 we read,

> For I have been informed concerning you, my brethren, by Chloe's people, that there are quarrels among you. Now I mean this, that each

one of you is saying, "I am of Paul, and I of Apollos, and I of Cephas, and I of Christ." Has Christ been divided? Paul was not crucified for you, was he? Or were you baptized in the name of Paul? I thank God that I baptized none of you except Crispus and Gaius, so that no one would say you were baptized in my name. Now, I did also baptize the household of Stephanas; beyond that, I do not know whether I baptized any other. For Christ did not send me to baptize, but to preach the gospel, not in cleverness of speech, so that the Cross of Christ would not be made void.

Some in the Corinth church were arguing in favor of their favorite leader, presumably the one who led them to faith in Christ and afterward baptized them in water. They were comparing personalities, strengths, and gifts. But Paul restrains them from comparing him with the others. Christ had to be their focal point. He reminds them that each leader had his own calling and assignment and was not to be compared with others. Each one possessed value and stood on his own merits. When we compare God's servants in an unhealthy fashion, we literally bring division to the local church. There is no place for "preacher religion"!

Could it be the Lord is calling you to help a given church reach its divine potential? Comparing churches to churches or a pastor with other pastors is not an apples-to-oranges ideal. Outside of your salvation, selecting a local church is one of the most important decisions you and your family will ever make. I beg you. Don't leave because the grass looks greener on the other side. "We are His people and the sheep of His pasture" (Ps. 100:3b). Make sure you end up in the right pasture!

Questions to Ponder

1. Why is it unwise to compare ourselves to others?

2. Read 2 Corinthians 10:12–13 again. What was Paul's struggle?

3. How does comparing churches cause some to leave a given church?

37

The Ten Suggestions

$\mathcal{I}$ still remember my dad's generation (builders) talking about couples who "shacked up." To them, it was both disgraceful and unacceptable. To "shack up" meant that a man and woman lived together without being married. And not only did church folks feel this way; it was an overall cultural mind-set of the 1950s and '60s. As I recall, the Ten Commandments were posted in our public school classrooms during those same years. We understood these commandments were, in effect, boundaries. God gave the Commandments not to limit our joy but to protect us. He told Israel, in essence, "Live within these boundaries and you will find life to be rewarding and fulfilling. Live outside these boundaries and you will experience heartache and pain." During the past five decades, we have witnessed a move away from these commandments. They are largely viewed as suggestions in contemporary culture. As a matter of fact, many who abhorred shacking up in the 1950s and '60s moved in with members of the opposite sex in the 1980s and '90s! In a day of lost pensions and scaled-down Social Security checks, it became all too easy to concede formerly held convictions.

The Pew Research Center, in a recent poll, learned that most Americans, ages eighteen to twenty-nine, say it's acceptable for an unmarried couple to live together. Moral absolutes have been traded for relativism. In other words, what is right is determined not by the absolutes of God's Word, but by the opinions of individuals. "What's right is what's right for me" remains the foundational premise of relativism. Relativism and humanism lock arms to create a me-centered viewpoint that exalts mankind as "little gods." Like the nation of Israel during the times of the judges, our nation also has embraced relativism. The very last verse of Judges describes the state of Israel in approximately 1030 BC and our current state: "In those days there was no king in Israel; everyone did what was right in his own eyes" (21:25). According to the dictionary, relativism is the doctrine that knowledge, truth, and morality exist in relation to culture, society, and historical context and are not absolute. The danger of relativism is found in its source. Right and wrong is determined by the individual instead of God.

Christians believe that God's moral code, revealed in his Word, is nonnegotiable. Those who reject absolutism, then, are left to their own evil devices. We see this poignantly illustrated in Genesis 11, which describes the motivation that drove construction crews to build the Tower of Babel. In essence, what they were saying was, "We're going to build this tower regardless of what God thinks." Rebellion ruled the day. An anti-God sentiment settled upon the builders, led by the tyrant Nimrod, and God had to shut the project down. Our righteous God will not be mocked! Centuries later, the prophet Isaiah described yet another godless generation this way: "Woe to those who call evil good, and good evil; who substitute darkness for light and light for darkness; who substitute bitter for sweet and sweet for bitter. Woe to those who are wise in their own eyes and clever in their own sight" (5:20–21).

Any culture that renounces the authoritative Word of God as its standard by which to live always plunges into a sinkhole of immorality. Uncontrolled fleshly desires demand physical gratification. In the book of Judges, Samson becomes "exhibit A" regarding this truth. This much-loved judge did that which was right in his own eyes. Immorality blinded him spiritually, which led to his physical blindness and ultimately ended his life. As previously stated, any culture that rejects the absolute truths of God's Word always experiences a moral landslide. An internal rot begins to eat away at the moral fiber of that nation. Moral challenges facing the Church today include in part:

1. *Cohabitation.* It seems incongruous to me that couples will sign jointly for a thirty-year mortgage but will not marry. Are they more committed to a mortgage than to one another?
2. *Premarital sex.* Has God changed his mind about sex before marriage? Hardly.
3. *Pornography.* One-third of all internet surfers regularly pull up graphic websites. This number includes Christians as well.
4. *Homosexuality.* Same-sex relationships/marriages are getting more exposure on television commercials, movies (including Hallmark), and of course, the internet. To be sure, the LGBTQ community is gaining recognition.
5. *Abortion.* Roe vs. Wade has still not been overturned, even though opposing political parties have resided in the White House. However, recent Guttmacher Center Research indicates that the number of abortions has fallen to lower levels since the procedure became legal in 1973. This comes after 50 million abortions between 1973 and 2011. Still, one is too many.

In 1 Corinthians 6:10–11 Paul renounces several lifestyles.

> Do you not know that the unrighteous will not inherit the kingdom of God? Do not be deceived, neither fornicators, nor idolaters, nor adulterers, nor effeminate, nor homosexuals, nor thieves, nor the covetous, nor drunkards, nor revilers, nor swindlers, will inherit the kingdom of God. Such were some of you, but you were washed, but you were sanctified, but you were justified in the Name of the Lord Jesus Christ, and in the Spirit of our God.

Paul does not list these sins in any given order of severity. And he makes it clear that all of these sins can be forgiven—"such *were* some of you." These sins were rampant across the Roman Empire, and again Paul describes lifestyles, not occasional lapses into the respective sins. Basically, the apostle makes it clear these sins should not be named among those who claim Christ as Savior. Born-again people are called to a higher level of life and conduct. As salt and light, they stem the tide of culture, not vice versa.

Remember, Christians are not culture-driven, but Word-driven. The Church is called upon to show people a better way without becoming combative and judgmental. Christian parents have to stand in the gap with unconditional love and continued godly instruction regarding moral issues. They need to teach their children it's wrong to sleep with someone they're not married to. Encourage them to be virgins on their wedding night. Discuss why they should be married and afterward live with their mate. Tell them that abortion is not birth control, but the killing of unborn babies. Insist that marriage is the union of one man and one woman for life. And warn them the enemy will try to bring same-sex attractions into their lives; therefore, teach them to grow up cultivating healthy boy-girl relationships. These are absolutes supported by God's Word. Christians and local churches need to hold true to these wonderful absolutes given by God, not to steal their joy, but to keep them healthy and godly.

I love how the apostle Paul described the principle of godly perpetuity as it pertained to young Timothy: "For I am mindful of the sincere faith within you, which first dwelt in your grandmother Lois, and your mother Eunice, and I'm sure that is in you as well" (2 Tim. 1:5). And here's where many part with local churches. If our youth do not understand the nonnegotiability of these truths, they may fall into the snare of cultural influence when they grow older. It appears many have.

Historically, the Church has been known for dealing with the "whats" and not the "whys." I have just listed five "whats"—cohabitation, premarital sex, pornography, homosexuality, and abortion. These are five of the ten lifestyles discussed in 1 Corinthians 6:10. Should pastors today shy away from preaching absolutes? Of course not! Clarion calls must be sounded. Warnings must be given. Eternal souls are at stake. The Bible clearly opposes these lifestyles. And pastors everywhere struggle with how to confront these issues in love.

One Sunday, two transgender men attended our morning service. They sat in the second row, close to the stage. All eyes were on the two interlopers. Their female attire was colorful and flashy, and understandably, the spectacle interrupted the service. I was perfectly fine and even thankful for the two being present; that is, until one of the men began touching the other below the belt. I prayed for wisdom and made my move to bring redirection. Standing behind the two, I put my hand on their shoulders and leaned in so those around me could not hear. I said, "Guys, we're so glad you're with us, but I'm going to ask you to keep your hands to yourself. And by the way, if you were a married man and woman, I'd be doing the same thing. This is not the place for that." Immediately both apologized for their actions. After the service was over, I bolted toward the two men and said, "I hope you have no hard feelings, and I hope you'll come back." They were both kind and thanked me. A visiting couple inadvertently overheard the entire conversation that morning, and decided to make Hope Community their new church! They saw grace in action!

Here's my point: The "what" (transgender lifestyle) was obvious. The "why" was left to explain. The church's ready answer is "sin." It hit me like a ton of bricks. Those two knew in their hearts that what they were doing was wrong. However, they did not need to be rebuked or shamed. They needed a Christian who weeps over the lost to explain to them that God offered a better way through the Cross. They needed forgiveness, not judgment. You see, regardless of our sin, we already stand judged! "What" they were doing was sinful. That goes without saying. "Why" they were cross-dressing needed to be explored. I have come to understand that if we, through brokenness, love people and desire to see them come into newness of life, must be willing to major on the "whys" of sin and not stand in judgment on the specific sins themselves. Keep reading before you shut down! That memorable Sunday service tested my motivation as a pastor.

We pastors who tend to be image-conscious have to be willing to get dirty. It's in the trenches of sin, the hog pens, if you please, where we need to not only discuss the "whats," but also be willing to explain the "whys" of sinful behavior. In this case, those two young men needed someone through tears to ask them "why" they felt the need to express themselves in this manner. We need to protect the dignity of those who enter our church doors while at the same time exploring deeply rooted issues in the lives of broken people.

We give first time moms at Hope Community Church what we call a "shower table." A beautifully decorated table is placed in the lobby and everyone is given a list of baby needs. Usually, gifts are piled high as we celebrate a new life. Unwed mothers also are honored. We have been accused of overlooking sin. However, this happy time allows us to welcome new life while at the same time showing the love of Christ to a perhaps frightened young lady who faces an uncertain future. After all, the new arrival cannot be blamed for parental indiscretions. Then too, the church may be honored to conduct a wedding in the future!

And speaking of potential weddings, perhaps more than ever before, unmarried couples attend our churches, and many have children—his, hers, and theirs. When any culture strays from moral absolutes, cohabitation accelerates. Living together apart from marriage results either from couples getting burned in previous relationships or viewing their choice as a trial run. Engaging in sexual intercourse is a foregone conclusion. Who are we kidding? Right? Two healthy individuals will not—cannot—abstain. Now that I've laid that to rest, let's explore the church's response to these precious couples.

If a church sees itself primarily as a place where "sinners" must be policed and held at bay, then most likely, couples will feel judged and ostracized. After all, the church must maintain its righteous standards! Pastors are challenged with what to do. To do nothing constitutes compromise to many; however, to assume a corrective posture most always drives said couples out the door, never to return.

There's nothing easy about this dilemma, but we must ask ourselves, "What is the purpose of the church?" Our answer will determine our response to couples "living in sin." Some pastors refuse to marry couples already living together, or either they insist that the man or woman moves out until the wedding day. My general feeling is that we get couples moving toward a righteous conclusion, all the while leaving the specifics up to the ongoing work of the Holy Spirit. Working with couples during these times must be seen as an event in progress. If salvation is both an event and a process, then God surely must view our pre-salvation days in the same way. To me, my emphasis during these times is to reach God's intention instead of my preference. Legislated righteousness may work initially, but it strips the spirit and life out of any ministry.

If we view the local church as a hospital for broken lives, and see it as God's sole redemptive agency to build healthy families, we will take a proactive role in helping couples move toward marriage. To me, it is incongruous to tell someone, "You're in sin, and the Lord is not pleased with you," and then offer no righteous resolve. How many couples have left churches angry and feeling condemned? Do you remember the three-point sermon about Samson (chapter 21)? Do you recall that point IV, the conclusion, was left out? We need to give people Jesus, sin's remedy. May God help us!

If we see the church as a place for only the righteous to assemble, or we see our role as punitive, we cannot possibly wonder why couples leave. Of course, we need not place these couples in spiritual leadership, but we can give them first-class treatment by honoring their significance as human beings (see chapter 40). Churches that feel it their responsibility to "contend for the faith"—albeit misled—will always ignore human need in lieu of perceived righteousness. Perhaps we need to rethink what compromise looks like. Those same churches will, in the aftermath, say, "We maintained our purity." However, given time, the church may lessen its influence in the community and another life may forever disdain local church ministry.

Most churches know how to throw a party. At Hope Community, we've learned how to "throw a wedding." When couples already living together sit under the Gospel and feel the love of God and the people, along with the tug of the Holy Spirit, one of the first things I hear is, "We need to get married." Spirit conviction wins the day!

What's my point? Allow the Holy Spirit to do his perfect work in transforming sinners into saints. "Nevertheless I tell you the truth; it is expedient for you that I go away; for if I go not away, the Comforter will not come unto you, but if I depart, I will send Him unto you. And when He is come, He will reprove (convince) the world of sin, and of righteousness, and of judgment" (John 16:7–8). When "He reproves the world (couple) of sin," we remain on standby to turn our Sunday morning service into a wedding ceremony. Afterward, we gather in the church cafe for a dynamite reception! The enemy gets a black eye, a couple invokes the blessings of God on their union, and a community at large sees grace in action. Church baby showers and weddings for those who missed God's original design validate the wonder and beauty of the Gospel. And factor into our annual budget!

Jesus said, "It is not the healthy who need a doctor, but the sick. I have not come to call the righteous, but sinners" (Mark 2:17). Can we ask the Holy Spirit to pull out root issues (whys), instead of always judging the "whats"? Unless one has grown calloused and reprobate (Rom. 1–2), the Holy Spirit is able to expose the "whys" and bring people to repentance. The Church majors on discussing sin, but in my opinion, fails in the area of bringing people from the "whats" to the "whys." Exposing sin is the Spirit's job; leading people from sin to complete healing and deliverance precludes our responsibility to make disciples. In other words, people need to be loved into the kingdom. I was! Think about it. You were too!

As Pastor Steven Furtick says, "People usually know what we (the Church) are against. We need to share the good news about what we are for!" People need to hear that the Lord is for them, not against them. He hates what sin does to people, but passionately loves the sinner. Back to those two young men. Their transgender lifestyle had an underlying cause and effect. The Holy Spirit wanted to expose their sin and subsequently show them a better way. For sure, the five sins listed above need to be addressed. Those who find themselves caught up in any one of these lifestyles need to repent and forsake their ways. God is willing to forgive! Conversely, we, the Church, need to avoid assuming an attack mode by strictly emphasizing the "whats." We need to invite the Holy Spirit to go beyond the surface pain of what we do and reveal the deeper pain that the enemy of our soul inflicts upon all of us as we move through life.

Yes, sin is sin. Make no mistake about it. But when we come across with anger and judgmental hearts, we push people away from the only source that can save and deliver. We have the "whats" down pat. Now, can we invite the Holy Spirit to pull out the "whys," believing him to complete redemption's work? And can we further remind true Christians that the Church must hold its standards high while at the same time loving people out of their sin into the arms of a loving Savior who waits to show them a better way?

I recently heard a radio minister say while preaching on 1 Corinthians 6:10–11, "Hell will burn hot for those who practice these lifestyles." His voice was anger-filled and his preaching style was condemnatory. His accusatory manner, I'm sure, pushed away anyone struggling with these lifestyle issues. At one point he said, "Those fags in North Carolina..." And off went the radio! What did he do? He declared war on those involved in this sin and rendered void the only saving grace available to them. How sad! I love what David Wilkerson said many years ago, "God calls believers to a baptism of anguish to fervently pay for the recovery of a nation." He encouraged preachers to never deliver sermons that had not been wept over.

Dear Church, can we get back to weeping over sin instead of exploiting it? Those ensnared by the enemy will continue to leave our churches. We must truly believe it when we say, "Hate the sin and love the sinner." The difference could mean pulling captives out of the snare of the devil versus pushing those far from God out the door. This is not in support of cheap grace, but realizing that all of us stand in need of saving grace. Harsh evangelistic tactics only serve to build higher walls instead of bridges into the lives of those closest to eternity and being forever lost. Let's give everyone in the sphere of our influence a reason to stay in a local church.

Questions to Ponder

1. What are other examples of absolutes in Scripture?

2. What happens to any culture that rejects moral absolutes?

3. Why were the Ten Commandments given in the first place?

4. What does it mean when we say, "Hate the sin and love the sinner"?

5. The author says, "The Church deals primarily with the 'whats' of sin, but fails in the area of the 'whys.'" What is your understanding of this comment?

6. Why do immoral lifestyles cause people to leave churches?

38

He Said, She Said

I believe in prophetic ministry. However, I have struggled with the Church's sometimes over-the-top teachings on the prophetic during the past twenty-five years. Can I be honest with you? I never heard the phrases "prophetic word" or "prophetic preaching" used in our circles until the latter part of last century. I was perfectly comfortable with the phrase "the preached Word."

Then, as if a new doctrine hit the church scene, many began talking about "the prophetic" as if God was introducing something new. I'm not trying to be disrespectful or snide; I have really struggled with what many dub the "prophetic movement." I understand that God moves in "seasons," but I also believe the prophetic has suffered much abuse and misuse. And I have never heard so much ridiculous teaching and seen so much hypersensationalism done in the name of the Lord.

How many offerings have I sat through that used some aspect of the prophetic to move people to give? I do not see myself as a close-minded preacher, but I admit, I am squeamish when it comes to the prophetic. I personally believe many people have used the Lord's name to scratch their "hyperspiritual itches" and to elevate them "above what is written" (1 Cor. 4:6). Remove humility from prophetic ministry, and you have a train wreck. I tire of the showmanship and attention-seeking that accompanies a lot of prophetic meetings. Yes, God does speak to individuals, and yes, there are times when prophetic words are welcome, but too much of the time, the "prophetic word" smacks of a "pathetic word," when individuals are highlighted and "the testimony of Jesus, who is the spirit of prophecy" (Rev. 19:10) is sidelined.

I understand the prophetic gift involves "seeing," but the pronoun *I* is used way too much for my comfort. If truth be told, my hesitancy to embrace certain aspects of the modern prophetic movement, goes all the way back to 1972 when my mother passed away after a long, grueling sickness. A well-meaning man whom I admired in the faith came to me and said, "The Lord said, 'I'm going to heal your mother. Watch me perform my wonders.'" I was overwhelmed with emotion and accepted the man's "word from the Lord" to be true. Three weeks later, Mom died. I was a fairly new believer, and her death shook me to my core, emotionally and spiritually. I suppose it was this unfortunate incident that made me suspicious of the prophetic. However, I do not wish to throw the baby out with the bathwater. I'm being brutally honest, so wait before you judge me!

Ephesians 4:11a says, "And He gave some as apostles, and some as prophets, and some as evangelists, and some as pastors and teachers." We refer to these offices as the "five-fold ministry." And I'm so thankful for these wonderful gifts that Christ gave to his Church. We need all of them functioning in a biblically sound manner if we are to come into the fullness of the stature of Christ: "For the equipping of the saints for the work of service to the building up of the body of Christ" (11b). And so, we acknowledge the office of prophet. However, unless these offices and their functions are properly taught and understood, then we are likely to have a "five-fold feud" on our hands! By the way, the original manuscripts combine the offices of pastor-teacher, often referring to only four offices.

I usually explain the individual roles this way:

- The Apostle: to send
- The Prophet: to see
- The Evangelist: to speak
- The Pastor: to tend
- The Teacher: to teach (of course!)

I'm going to go out on a limb and say based on personal experience these five offices, to work effectively and to stay in balance, need
to channel through the office of pastor. After all, it is the pastor who
gets in the trenches with the sheep! The other four offices should
humbly come into line with the pastor's ministry, as he, under God,
leads each local church.

This is the pattern I see in the New Testament, as revealed in
Paul's writings to the various churches. And of course, these offices
can and do overlap one another. Neither time nor space will allow me
to cover apostles, evangelists, pastors, and teachers, so let me get back
to the office of prophet. Are there prophets in today's Church? Of
course! "Now at this time some prophets came down from Jerusalem
to Antioch. One of them named Agabus, began to indicate by the
Spirit that there would certainly be a great famine all over the world.
And this took place in the reign of Claudius" (Acts 11:27–28). The
abovementioned famine later embraced the entire known world at
the time. These were, in fact, new covenant prophets!

However, please understand that prophets in today's church
are different from the prophets mentioned in the Old Testament.
Prophets of renown—Samuel, Isaiah, Jeremiah, Ezekiel, Elijah,
Elisha—*foretold* what God was doing, especially pertaining to Israel.
They were protectors of the Covenant and foretold the coming of the
Messiah with amazing and detailed accuracy. Prophets today *forthtell*
what God has already proclaimed in His Word because the Canon of
Scripture—the Bible—is closed. God has already told us everything
we need to know as it pertains to our salvation and those things yet
to come upon the earth. And like the prophets mentioned in Acts
11:27–28, God uses prophets today to warn of things to come—
those things related to sin and judgment. Perhaps the prophet Amos
said it best: "Surely the Lord God does nothing, unless He reveals
His secret counsel to His servants the prophets" (3:7). This time-
tested verse balances the "foretelling" with the "forth-telling" aspects
of prophetic ministry.

Always remember, the acid test of a true prophet is that his prophecies come true. I still struggle with men and women of God who insist
on carrying titles. We have become both image and title crazy.

I'm also very concerned about the abuses I've personally witnessed and heard in regards to the gift of prophecy as discussed in 1 Corinthians 12. "Now there are varieties of gifts...and to each one is given the manifestation of the Spirit for the common good...to another prophecy" (verses 4, 7, and 10). Paul wrote to the Church at Corinth to correct abuses that had developed while employing the gift of prophecy and the other gifts mentioned in chapter 12. And today, the potential for abuse is present as well. Pastors have the responsibility to make sure these gifts bring edification and comfort, not confusion and strife. "All things have to be done decently and in order" (1 Cor. 14:40).

A wonderful gift in the wrong hand (heart) becomes a sideshow attraction that draws attention away from Christ to the individual. All attention and adoration goes to Jesus! Only him! Now that I have introduced my concerns surrounding the prophetic ministry, allow me to point out seventeen principles, teachings, and warnings that I believe should guide prophetic emphases in the local church.

1. People often speak out of their soul instead of by the Spirit of God. I call them "Pentecostal well-wishers." The man who prophesied to me about my dying mother fit into this category. He meant well; however, his best intentions were misled. He wanted to see my mom healed, but allowed his emotions to override what the Spirit was really saying. And if individuals have broken, unhealed areas in their soul—mind, will, and emotions—they are likely to speak through those "filters." Beware! God, of course, uses imperfect vessels to speak in today's Church; however, we dare not filter the intended message through wounded emotions. In the past, when I preached through anger, everyone suffered! Love has to be the motivating force in all we do.

2. Individuals with mental health issues, who are emotionally unstable, or cognitively challenged, often use the prophetic to exaggerate their importance or to draw attention to themselves. They function as engines not hitting on all six cylinders. In my opinion, these individuals must be redi-

rected away from public ministry, toward more behind-the-scenes types of ministry.

3. Frankly, the prophetic gift is perhaps the most likely to be abused. It seems that everything now has a prophetic angle to it—prophetic poetry, drawings, art, prayers, songs, and even choruses. What? Why do we have to use the word *prophetic* to describe innate gifts or interests?

4. Many who prophesy lack knowledge of God's Word, are spiritually shallow or pseudo-spiritual, regularly gossip, walk in unforgiveness, operate in pride or false humility, or sow discord in the church. Only consistent Christian character validates those who operate in the prophetic, or any of the gifts, for that matter.

5. Believers who tend to be "loose cannons," refusing to submit to pastoral authority and instruction, forfeit their right to express any prophetic gifts inside them. In summary, those who refuse to come under spiritual authority, disqualify themselves from speaking in the church. In the same way, women who function outside of healthy spiritual order in their home need to understand that God recommends a "meek and quiet spirit" (1 Pet. 3:4) that submits to his revealed plan.

6. Many prophetic words do not line up with God's Word. Some even contradict God's Word and/or obvious biblical principles. We are called to judge the validity of any prophetic word.

7. Prophetic words should always be unto edification or bring comfort (1 Cor. 14:12). They should never be used as weapons of mass destruction!

8. Some use the gift to "read others' mail." God never tattletales on one kid to another! Prophetic words are separate from words of knowledge or words of wisdom, as these gifts usually operate in obscurity and confidentiality.

9. Too many treat prophetic words like a crystal ball—reading the future. Always remember, the gift of prophecy, when used by impure, self-serving vessels, closely parallels the

travesty of divination, which aligns with enemy strategy. One of the most dangerous realities happens when individuals who at one time operated accurately in the prophetic word, and subsequently turned apostate. The gift inside them transferred to the demonic realm. Currently, hundreds of psychic hotlines exist for those seeking answers to life's questions and dilemmas. My guess is that a good number of these "readers" previously operated in the genuine prophetic word and sadly were somehow wounded in the house of God and allowed offenses to make them rebellious. You remember that "rebellion is as the sin of witchcraft" (1 Sam. 15:23). Operating in the gifts of the Holy Spirit remains a high and holy opportunity. And an awestruck responsibility.

10. Prophetic words are not given to provide direction, only confirmation. God does not operate on a third-party basis. He's not going to tell Bill to tell Bob to tell me! What a beautiful experience it is to have someone confirm what God has already told us! We all have direct access to God's throne and should cultivate hearts (ears) that listen to God's voice.

11. Prophetic words should not be elevated above God's Word. I've known people who kept dated journals of personal prophecies and relied on them more than trusting God's Word.

12. The Scriptures nowhere support the practice of giving "personal prophecies," or what I call "assembly line prophetic words." Inflated egos, pride, manipulative people, and self-indulgent attitudes fill our churches when people are allowed to operate in this vein. I've seen churches suffer serious setbacks by allowing this self-serving practice to continue.

13. Some who refer to having a prophetic anointing really have the "gift of suspicion"! This very misdirected "gift" can bring much harm into any situation.

14. Some overlook the fact that words of knowledge and words of wisdom are often given as prophetic words. They are dif-

ferent in purpose and operation and never meant for public expression. The gifts of prophecy, tongues, and interpretation of tongues are the only verbal-public gifts discussed in 1 Corinthians. And remember, tongues manifested in the public worship service must always be followed by an interpretation.

15. As a general rule, so-called prophetic worship songs are given for individual edification and private times of praise, not for public worship. I've been amazed at how "prophetic singers" attempt to lead entire congregations of worshipers, without realizing that the only one singing is the leader. They are an audience of one! Entire congregations are reduced to spectators. Some well-meaning worship leaders are misdirected and/or oblivious to the very people they are trying to lead into the presence of God. Worship leaders would do well to remember that the object of our worship is Jesus, and the ideal of worship is to get as many involved as possible in the act of worship. So-called prophetic worship automatically disengages the leader from those he strives to lead! There are exceptions, but very few indeed! Plus, worship leaders should step up to the mic only after they have been filled. At that point, they become conduits through which the anointing flows. That anointing is what draws the people into a time of worship. Full vessels lead parched souls without placing guilt and shame upon the gathered church.

16. What is prophetic preaching? Not all biblical passages carry prophetic implications. Paul told Timothy, "Preach the Word" (2 Tim. 4:2). He did not say, "Prophesy the Word." I may be splitting hairs, but the difference again remains the difference between Christ-centered and messenger-centered ministry. My friend, when rightly divided, the Word speaks for itself! We don't "read into" the Word; we allow the Word to "read us." And this truth leads me to my last observation.

17. Some preaching referred to as prophetic preaching simply draws analogies or embraces allegories used to teach a

higher principle, or one that hides beneath the surface of a Bible story. Such preaching also draws from types and shadows revealed in a given passage. Let me give an example of each:

Analogy (metaphors). Proverbs 13:14 says, "The teaching of the wise is a fountain of life." This metaphor compares wise teaching to a flowing fountain. Sometimes when individuals give prophetic words, they use colorful imagery to share God's message. This type of prophetic ministry is totally subjective, leaving the message open-ended and subject to personal interpretation. I for one, am cautioned to not build my future on "I see" or "I think" or "Take this for what it's worth." I need something more solid! How many people have walked away from having received a prophetic word of such a general nature, asking themselves, "What did that mean?" I have, realizing what was spoken could have been understood in any number of ways! Or misunderstood!

Allegory. The Bible contains several allegories. An allegory is a literary work in which the characters and events are symbolic of a deeper moral or spiritual truth. For example, the Song of Solomon is viewed as an allegory by both Jewish and Christian scholars. One says it's an allegory of God's love for Israel. The other says it's an allegory about Christ's love for the Church. Still, others believe it's an allegory about married love. Prophetic words based on allegorical passages are also left up to private interpretation. They, too, are subjective and need to be received with caution!

Types and shadows. Acts 27 records the story of Paul sailing from Caesarea to Rome when he encounters a shipwreck. When the 276 passengers and crew announce they are jumping ship, Paul tells them if they remain in the ship, their lives will be spared. "Then Paul said to the centurion and the soldiers, 'Unless those men stay with the ship, you cannot be saved.'" The ship, then, is a type of the Church or "staying with the Lord." This type of biblical preaching is challenging because it, too, leaves room for personal interpretation. So what is the drawback on prophetic ministry that builds on analogies, allegories, and types and shadows?

Always remember. We need to draw on a literal interpretation of Scripture that requires full disclosure of the text and minimizes temptations to "read into the text" what may or may not be there. This is also the drawback to preaching topical series! Some search for Scriptures to support their erroneous thinking or personal opinions. This is dangerous. Prophetic words that employ any of these three comparative genres have to be time tested and weighed in light of a deeper, more solid biblical interpretation. I sure would not build an entire church service or more important, a life decision on prophetic words that leave themselves open to interpretations that are general, not specific in their intent. Such prophetic activity may seem good at the time; however, we must build our lives on "The Word," not "a word."

As I write, I understand my potential for being misunderstood. However, if prophetic ministry is allowed to run rampant outside the guidelines of biblical authority, the chances for confusion and division remain a constant threat. And the gift of prophecy must never be allowed to get out of balance with the other ministry gifts. Entire services that feature only prophetic ministry open the door to extremes that highlight imbalanced and overzealous believers. In my experience, nothing overrides the preaching of God's Word.

The preceding ideas about the prophetic in today's church should by no means be seen as a comprehensive treatment. Volumes have been written about each of the above guidelines. This summary simply provides a general overview for those who have perhaps been confused (like me) regarding the intents and purposes for which the prophetic gifts should operate in today's Church. Sadly, I've seen churches fall apart because prophetic extremes were allowed to infiltrate the congregation. Fallout was terrible, and people left because of abuses driven by arrogance and imbalanced teaching. May God help us deliver a Gospel message that is clearly presented and points people to the Cross of Christ.

Questions to Ponder

1. What are your personal reservations, if any, regarding the contemporary prophetic ministry?

2. What is the difference between "The Word" and "a word"?

3. Review the author's seventeen teachings and warnings. Which ones align with your concerns? Which ones do you need further clarification on? Discuss your questions/concerns with your pastor.

39

Keeping Score

After sin entered the human race in the Garden of Eden, Adam and Eve and everyone born after them have suffered from relationship breakdowns. Relationships were one of the hardest hit areas of life. Stories of people who refused to forgive their perpetrators, who held grudges, and who grew bitter fill the pages of human history. Indeed, many still refuse to forgive those who have brought offense and pain into their lives. They keep a running total of wrongs done. And unfortunately, this also happens inside local churches, often causing an exodus.

The *New Living Translation* renders 1 Corinthians 13:5 this way: "Love keeps no record when it has been wronged." Agape love, or God's love, produces amnesia. To God, confessed sin is forgiven sin! Psalm 103:12 says, "As far as the east is from the west, so far has He removed our transgressions from us." In Isaiah 43:25, the prophet writes, "I, even I, am the one who wipes out your transgressions for my own sake. And I will not remember your sins." Isaiah 37:18 says, "It is You who has kept my soul from the pit of nothingness. For you have cast all my sins behind your back." Psalm 130:3 asks, "If you Lord, should mark iniquities, O Lord, who could stand?" Sin placed under the blood of Jesus Christ is gone and forgotten!

Often, we hear people say, "I'll forgive, but I'll never forget." I used to subscribe to this way of thinking until one day the Lord challenged my attitude. A lot of Christians buy into this unscriptural teaching. In reality, many times it's justification for continued grudge-holding.

Forgive and forget. Is it possible? Yes and no! All of us have been hurt by someone—probably more than once. The prophet Zechariah said it this way: "I was wounded in the house of my friends" (13:6). Someone said, "I'm not God, so it's impossible for me to forget hurtful people and situations in my life. I don't go brain-dead when I forgive. I still remember the details!" That's not completely true. Given time, none of us with 100 percent accuracy remember the details of our lives. However, we do assign an emotion to everything significant that happens to us. When offenses come our way, it's not our spirit man who gets wounded; it's our soul man. Our soul—mind, will, and emotions—reacts negatively during times of offense. Again, we don't remember facts. We assign negative emotions to those facts.

Like people in general, Christians get hurt along life's journey, and sometimes even in the local church. Jesus warned us in Matthew 24:10 that offenses will accelerate in the last days: "And then many will be offended." However, we possess the indwelling Spirit who helps us righteously process those negative experiences that afflict our soul. Through prayer God assigns new interpretations to our negative experiences. What people sometimes do for evil, God reverses for our good—and theirs!

Do we forget when we forgive people who bring offense and emotional pain into our lives? Of course not! But God graciously pulls the pain out of the situation by giving us a healthier interpretation of the facts. Offenses always bring emotional pain, but when we allow God to exchange our pain by his power, he assigns a new interpretation of what happened and the negative emotional residue fades into the past. In this sense, we can forgive and forget! An overview of the life of Joseph, recorded in Genesis 37–50 provides a perfect illustration of this wonderful reality!

For our purposes, let's look at the events recorded in chapter 50 only. Now second in command in the land of Egypt, Joseph says something to his brothers that explains this process. As you may recall, he had been terribly mistreated by his brothers. At seventeen, he was cast into a pit—probably an empty, deep well—because of their anger and jealousy. Later he was sold to a caravan of Ishmaelite traders on their way to Egypt. During the next thirteen years, he faced his share of trials, but in the plan and purpose of God, he ultimately triumphed and ended up as Egypt's prime minister.

Psalm 105:17–19 describes his plight. "He (God) sent a man before them, even Joseph, who was sold for a servant: Whose feet they hurt with fetters: he was laid in iron: Until the time that his word came: the Word of the Lord tried him." I'm sure Joseph experienced many anxious days and anger during those trying years. Eventually, a severe famine in their homeland drove his brothers to Egypt to seek relief. Joseph, of course, recognized his siblings, but withheld his identity long enough to weigh their motives. A game of cat and mouse centering on his beloved brother, Benjamin followed, until Joseph became convinced of his brothers' changed hearts. When life brings pain and unfair days, we have two choices. We either respond negatively or positively. We get bitter or better. One definition of forgiveness is "relinquishing our right to get even or to take matters into our own hands." In the soul realm, Joseph perhaps had every right to punish his brothers. Instead, he chose to embrace a righteous interpretation of the facts.

"As for you, you meant evil against me, but God meant it for good in order to bring about this present result, to preserve many people alive" (verse 20). That was Joseph's defining moment! A lot of people allow the inequities and hurts of life to become their defining moments. They make a cognitive choice not to forgive. In short, they assign negative emotions to what happened. Anger rules their lives. Remember, not forgiving is a choice! Obviously, Joseph remembered his brothers' harsh treatment years prior; however, he chose not to rehearse the details and to lay aside the emotional residue of his offense. In that respect, he was able to forgive and forget! When we place such matters in God's hands, it is possible to forgive those who sin against us. Forgiveness causes our memories to fade and our souls to heal. In a very real sense, we do forget. God heals our soul as we release our pain to him in prayer. The Holy Spirit heals our mind and emotions.

How do we know when we have truly forgiven someone? When the offense comes to mind, if indeed it does, and it no longer hurts.

The sting is gone! Prayer is therapeutic, and as we release those who hurt us, the Holy Spirit gives a new interpretation of the situation and eliminates the pain. Remember, Joseph had thirteen years to process his pain. You can bet that his initial decision to forgive his brothers (back when) still held pain. Eventually, total forgiveness erased his pain. Our spiritual forefathers referred to this process as "praying through." This is but one of the beautiful and practical aspects of our sanctification.

Before I conclude my thoughts on forgiveness, I wish to offer a partial theological treatise on how God forgives us. To fully experience the dynamics of forgiveness and forgetting, we need to understand the act of justification. Justification is God's act of declaring believing sinners righteous and acceptable in his sight. It is a legal term. Justification is possible because Christ has borne the sinner's sin on the Cross "and has been made unto him righteousness" (1 Cor. 1:30). Romans 3:24 says, "Being justified freely by his grace through the redemption that is in Christ Jesus."

Justification springs from the fountain of God's grace. "But when the kindness of God our Savior and his love for mankind appeared, he saved us, not on the basis of deeds which we have done in righteousness, but according to his mercy, by the washing of regeneration and renewing by the Holy Spirit" (Titus 3:4–5). For you see, Jesus satisfied all the demands of the Old Testament law. Justification is on the basis of faith, not by human merits or works. In this marvelous operation of God, the holy judge of the universe declares righteous the one who believes in Jesus.

Romans 8:31–34 says, "What then shall we say in response to these things? If God is for us, who can be against us? He who did not spare his own Son, but gave him up for us all—how will he not also, along with him, graciously give us all things? Who will bring any charge against those whom God has chosen? It is God who justifies. Why then is the one who condemned? No one. Christ Jesus who died—more than that who was raised to life—is at the right hand of God and is also interceding for us."

A justified believer emerges from God's great courtroom with a consciousness that another, his Substitute, has borne his guilt and that he stands without accusation before the bar of God. The believer is justified in Christ, and "there is now no condemnation for those who are in Christ Jesus" (Rom. 8:1). So if God for Christ's sake forgives us, we can forgive others. And if God looks upon us "just as if we never sinned," then we can look upon those who sin against us in like manner. It's all by his grace and empowerment.

The prophet Micah was outspoken and fearless in announcing the iniquities of Judah. However, he ended his prophecy with these wonderful words:

> Who is a God like you, who pardons iniquity and passes over the rebellious act of the remnant of his possession? He does not retain his anger forever, because he delights in his unchanging love. He will again have compassion on us; he will tread our iniquities under his feet. Yes, you will cast all their sins into the depths of the sea. (7:18–19)

God does not keep score! When we repent of our sin and confess it, he casts it into his "sea of forgetfulness" to be remembered against us no more. Jesus made it clear: "Whenever you stand praying forgive; if you have anything against anyone, so that your Father who is in heaven will also forgive you your transgressions. But if you do not forgive, neither will your Father who is in heaven forgive your transgressions" (Mark 11:25–26). To forgive is a choice. The pain may still be felt, but your desire to forgive remains intact.

Have you embraced the "I'll forgive, but I won't forget" concept? Remember, God is able to help you assign a new, redemptive interpretation to your pain. Rejoice as he pulls the negative emotions out of the skewed details of your past. Approach your former nemesis, look him in the eyes, and give him a big hug (if only in your mind)! Jesus's unconditional love and God's act of pardon will cause you to love everyone! Do you remember the chorus "Old Time Religion"? One verse says, "It makes me love everybody." It's hard to love sometimes, but tell your soul man to line up. Emotions may still remain, but the spirit man wins! "The love of God has been poured out within our hearts through the Holy Spirit who was given to us" (Rom. 5:5).

Questions to Ponder

1. Can we truly forgive and forget those who bring pain into our lives? How?

2. What does the term *justification* mean?

3. In what sense is forgiveness a process?

4. How do we know when we have truly forgiven someone?

40

Bring Back Honor

In Luke 19, we read about a despised little man by the name of Zacchaeus. You've heard this story most of your Christian life and perhaps even sang about him as a child:

> Zacchaeus was a wee little man,
> and a wee little man was he.
> He climbed up in a sycamore tree,
> for the Lord he wanted to see.
> And when the Savior passed that way,
> He looked up in the tree and said,
> "Zacchaeus, you come down.
> For I'm going to your house today!
> For I'm going to your house today!"

When we planted Hope Community Church, my wife and I committed to making this church an "honoring community." By this, I mean we wanted to talk more about what we're "for" as Christians, more than what we're "against." It seems that in today's church we talk more about what's wrong than what's right. I'm not talking about sin; I'm talking about a lack of honor and respect in our culture that has, I'm afraid, spilled over into churches. We understand that man's problems trace back to the issue of sin, which originated in the Garden of Eden. Sin has taken a devastating toll on humanity. Everywhere we look, we see the terrible effects that sin plays on the stage of human history. The Church must continue to pray and act upon the fact that men are far from God and need to find new life in Christ.

Our message must remain intact. Sinners need to get hooked up with the Savior—Jesus Christ. This is nonnegotiable.

However, the church often takes a negative approach when communicating earth's most positive message! Perhaps we need to rethink our approach. We expect sinners to act like saints when their spiritual DNA dictates otherwise. Evangelicals have been known to assume an attack mode on sin and inadvertently struggle with "sinners versus their sin." We often make those outside our churches feel condemned and sadly even disdained because they either differ with our theology or they don't act like we do. Hidden away behind church doors are Christians who mix their message with self-righteous animosity. Believe me, no one attends church services to be told how bad he is and to be raked over the coals of legalistic injustice.

Yes, people need the Lord. Yes, they need to be saved. Yes, hell is a real place. Yes, continued lifestyles of sin eventually face God's righteous judgment. But no one needs to be disrespected or dishonored in the process. No one needs to feel insignificant or devalued. Jesus Christ still loves us regardless of our performance in the "sin department." That's the good news we call the Gospel!

I see an acceleration of dishonor and disrespect from the White House to our house! The Church of Jesus must stem this tide if we ever hope to impact our culture, communities, and children for Jesus. If a child grows up continually hearing how bad he is, how he will amount to nothing and being unreasonably punished, he might eventually make good on these self-fulfilling prophecies. We desperately need to create a culture of honor, for when we create a culture of honor and practice honor toward those around us, we will see the glory of God released in our churches. This story about Zacchaeus demonstrates that a little man who was despised by his community came to faith in Christ after Jesus showed him honor. He remains the poster boy for honor!

Zacchaeus's wounded heart and broken spirit were made glad by the man from Galilee who saw beyond his sordid reputation to his significance as a human being made in the image of God. Sin tarnishes our self-image; the grace of Jesus targets our innate significance. The Scriptures tell us that "there is none righteous, no, not one" (Rom. 3:10). We understand this; however, I'm not talking about our righteousness. I'm referring to our significance—our meaning or purpose. Significance refers to the potential of our personhood.

All of us were created by God "to matter." We are important in our own right, and we are placed upon this earth to help usher in God's kingdom. That's just one reason why abortion is such an atrocity. Insignificance, dishonor, and disrespect all kill our divine potential and rob us of an abundant life. Rob a man of his significance and you potentially keep him in a self-made prison of anger, unbelief, and low-living. Many people sit in churches week after week feeling they are undeserving of God's grace. When people realize their true significance in God's eyes, conversions accelerate. When we honor the unique personhood of all who enter our doors, we see God open their hearts to receive the goodness of God and his salvation. Honoring people helps take their eyes off their sin and place them on the Savior. The Spirit more easily convicts of sin when individuals feel that God loves them despite their behavior. Significance always trumps shame and inner turmoil. Now let's read the story of this infamous little man to see how Jesus showed him honor—a man whom many would say deserved no honor.

> Jesus entered Jericho and was passing through. A man was there by the name of Zacchaeus; he was a chief tax collector and was wealthy. He wanted to see who Jesus was, but because he was short he could not see over the crowd. So he ran ahead and climbed a sycamore fig tree to see him, since Jesus was coming that way. When Jesus reached the spot, he looked up and said to him, "Zacchaeus, come down immediately, I must stay at your house today." So he

came down at once and welcomed him gladly. All the people saw this and began to mutter, 'He has gone to be the guest of a sinner.' But Zacchaeus stood up and said to the Lord, "Look, Lord! Here and now I give half of my possessions to the poor, and if I have cheated anybody out of anything, I will give back four times the amount." Jesus said to him, "Today salvation has come to this house, because this man too is a son of Abraham. For the Son of man came to seek and to save the lost."

Zacchaeus had several things working against him. He was a tax collector for Rome. He superintended the other tax collectors—as the chief tax collector. He was wealthy. He overtaxed people and kept the overage. He lived very well with his ill-gotten gain. He was a fraud. He was hated, despised, always looking over his shoulder. Always in danger of assassination. In short, a cheat and a liar! And yet, before the day's end, this man of small stature would find himself transformed—converted by the grace of Jesus.

Jesus Christ honored, not the man's lifestyle, not his character, not his sin, but he called forth the man's excruciating need to experience forgiveness, love, and affirmation. Wherever the Gospel is preached, it draws out the needs of mankind that only Christ himself can address. That's one reason why negative preaching cannot bring forth positive results. When we use our pulpits to tell people how bad they are, how much God is displeased with them and to browbeat already defeated people, we do the Gospel message a gross disservice and injustice.

The Gospel should draw on the heartstrings of lost people, not beat them up with condemnation, guilt, and shame. The Gospel is good news, not bad news. Had Jesus not honored the much-hated tax collector, Zacchaeus, like he did but continued to address him on the same course that the townspeople were accustomed to, Zacchaeus potentially would never have come to faith. Note with me in verse 7 that the people were used to coming at Zacchaeus in a very dishonoring and self-righteous manner: "He (Jesus) has gone to be the guest of a sinner." His reputation preceded him, and his chances for reconciliation and a better life were minimized. The Spirit of God, by all indicators, was dealing with the heart and attitude of that little man, or he would not have been there in the first place.

Something inside the tax collector caused him to show up that day when he heard that Jesus was coming, and desperation for life change drove that little guy up a tree! What was going inside this wretched tax collector went way beyond natural curiosity. Jesus would testify later concerning Zacchaeus that "today salvation has come to his house" (verse 9). Something supernatural was pulling at his heartstrings. Jesus Christ honored the much-despised man. He honored him by informing the unsuspecting loner of his dinner plans. What's so significant about the Master inviting himself to dinner? The Son of God loved him for who he was, not what he was! Jesus showed him honor! This little man perhaps lived in a gated community, or at least a gated parcel of property with high fences around his home. He probably lived on the outskirts of town where human interaction was minimal. Where the taunts and threats of angry people could not be heard.

We can well imagine that nights were spent alone, and every night represented a new eternity for the little man who had no friends and the friends he did have were fair-weather—hearts as crooked as his and ready to sell one another down the river if it meant more corrupt wealth. Rome certainly did not care about Zacchaeus. If he were murdered, there were always others to take his place. Zacchaeus was disposable and a human target.

His dimly lit home would only intensify the darkness of his already broken life. Zacchaeus would later testify that money fell short of a meaningful life. A repentant heart testified, "Here and now I give half of my possessions to the poor, and if I have cheated anybody out of anything, I will pay back four times the amount" (verse 8).

The crowd that day directed a calculated slur against the Master when they said, "He has gone home to be the guest of a sinner" (verse 7). Comically, Jesus invited himself to Zacchaeus's home for dinner! While this may be frowned upon in modern-day life—viewed as socially inappropriate—the Master touched a heartstring that caused the little man to come alive on the inside. "You mean, you want to come to my house tonight? My house? You're coming to my house?" Jesus Christ, in a display of honor, overlooked what Zacchaeus did for a living to honor who he was! Jesus honored the man's personhood. When someone honors us, we open our hearts to him.

In today's church, if we will honor those God sends us, I'm convinced we will see more conversions to Christ than ever before. That's why we at Hope Community continually stress servant leadership that places the needs of others over ours. People are frantically searching for significance. "Most important of all, continue to show deep love for each other, for love covers a multitude of sins" (1 Pet. 4:8). Jesus Christ knows how to get your attention. He knows what pulls on your heartstring. He will address you at the point of what captures your heart's attention and draw you toward saving faith. Jesus turns significance into salvation!

Questions to Ponder

1. In what ways can the local church use negative means to communicate the Gospel?

2. What happens to people who feel insignificant or devalued?

3. How do we honor another's personhood?

4. Jesus won Zacchaeus by showing him honor. How does the Holy Spirit use the need for significance to touch hearts?

41

Both Born and Made

*L*eadership expert, John Maxwell, said many years ago, "If you think you're leading, but no one is following, then you are only taking a walk." Leaders have to be intentional. I firmly believe that people want to be led. They will become discouraged by leaders they deem ineffective. I used to teach high school English, and I remember my principal telling me, "Roger, if you don't have a plan, your students will!" And he was right. Pastors who exhibit weak leadership skills or who lead by malfeasance are subject to having strong personalities challenge or even usurp their pastoral authority.

Local churches don't grow arbitrarily; they require constant oversight and attention. Any church body that is healthy automatically grows. However, that body still needs a growth plan. That's where pastors come in! Effective, ongoing planning is required to keep local churches—the body—vibrant and moving forward. Perpetuity mandates consistent prayer, hard work, and administrative savvy. It takes relationship building. When a pastor gathers a unified servant leadership team around him, each one shares a vital role in the church's success. Servant leadership always trumps positional-driven ministry.

Admittedly, the coronavirus has negatively impacted local church outreach, but hopefully, leaders have used this time to sure up their infrastructure. Perhaps we need to revisit the prayer of Jabez: "Now Jabez called on the God of Israel, saying, 'Oh that you would bless me indeed, and enlarge my border, and that Your hand might be with me, and that You would keep me from harm that it may not pain me!" And God granted him what he requested" (1 Chron. 4:10). Dear pastor friend, during this time of uncertainty and pandemic-produced interruptions, pray like never before!

The apostle Paul said it this way:

> I planted, Apollos watered, but God was causing the growth. So then neither the one who plants nor the one who waters is anything, but God who causes the growth. Now he who plants and he who waters are one, but each will receive his own reward according to his own labor. For we are God's fellow workers; you are God's field, God's building. According to the grace of God which was given to me, like a wise master builder I laid a foundation, and another is building on it. But each man must be careful how he builds on it. For no man can lay a foundation other than the one which is laid, which is Jesus Christ. (1 Cor. 3:6–11)

Pastor, there's never time to coast. Local churches are living organisms and require regular sustenance. The enemy never takes a break, and neither can you. Like any organization, local churches rise and fall on leadership. And local pastors and other leaders all have a role to fill, according to the gifts and assignments inside them.

I personally believe leaders are both born and made. Let's look at the life of Jeremiah, the Old Testament's "weeping prophet." His call to leadership came while in the womb. He spent his life "on assignment." Jeremiah pronounced God's judgment upon the nation of Judah for their wickedness. He was concerned especially about their false and insincere worship and failure to trust Yahweh in national affairs. He also renounced social injustice, proclaiming that the people would suffer famine, foreign conquest, plunder, and captivity in a land of strangers. Leadership, it seems, is a lifelong pursuit. Good leaders are ever-learning, developing, and maturing in their call. "Now the word of the Lord came to me saying, 'Before I formed you in the womb, I knew you, and before you were born I consecrated you. I have appointed you a prophet to the nations'" (1:4–5). In verse 10, he receives his marching orders: "To pluck up and to break down, to destroy and overthrow, to build and to plant." Sounds like what I do as a pastor!

Another word for *consecrated* is *called*. Jeremiah was called with a specific assignment. Leaders are assignment-driven. Effective leaders are also passion-driven. An assignment without passion spells indifference and lacks motivation. Passion without an assignment denotes a lack of vision. Leaders with only passion typically fly by the seat of their pants! They may be good preachers, but they also need to be good administrators, and good with organizational skills, or surround themselves with others who make up for their weaknesses.

Maxwell says, "A leader is one who knows the way, goes the way and shows the way." Local churches need pastors who understand vision and motivation. While I perfectly understand the necessity of maintaining momentum in the local church, I also realize how difficult it is. Effective leadership rides on the wings of momentum. As stated earlier, there's never time to coast. I recommend that pastors plan their ministry calendar at least one year in advance. Some pastors even plan their preaching schedule one year in advance. They, of course, remain flexible to the specific leadership of the Holy Spirit, listening to his voice and obeying his direction for each service.

Maxwell is one of God's leadership generals and has helped thousands of pastors and other leaders to identify and pull out their leadership skills and to help them improve in their areas of weakness. He says, "People buy into the leader before they buy into the vision." Pastors are God's visible representation chosen to lead local churches. The Holy Spirit is the "carrier of the glory." The pastor is the "carrier of the vision." Vision is character-driven, and that's why people relate to the man over the mission.

According to Smart Church Management, effective church leaders have certain traits that affect their interactions with others. Pastor friend, weigh in according to the following fourteen personal traits. Rejoice in your strengths and seek God's help for your liabilities. Effective leaders

1. carry influence,
2. function as big picture thinkers (visionaries),
3. believe the best in people,
4. possess credibility in the eyes of others,
5. work as teachers and mentors,
6. serve as master delegators,
7. empower others,
8. function as team players,
9. celebrate successes,
10. have balanced friendships,
11. have integrity in business practices,
12. have transparent accounting practices,
13. live according to a biblical code of conduct,
14. exhibit solid management practices.

The above list sounds more like a pastor-leader's job description. I don't know about you, but when I started out in ministry forty-three years ago, few, if any, older pastors were talking about these traits. It seems to me that many operated "on a wing and a prayer." There, of course, were exceptions, but for the most part, we were thrown into the ministry pond to sink or swim! I'm so thankful for the training that local church leaders are afforded today. We all understand that "it's not by our might, or by our power, but by the Spirit" (Zech. 4:6); however, we in cooperation with the Spirit of God appreciate any and all training opportunities we receive from proven pastors and other leaders. Thank God for the John Maxwells and other Christian leaders who make available heaven's resources, man's ingenuity and who encourage all of us to live and move in the Spirit's empowering. "In Him we live, we move and have our being" (Acts 17:28).

Questions to Ponder

1. Why is it necessary for churches and leaders to maintain momentum?

2. Leaders are both born and made. Do you agree or disagree? Why?

3. Leadership is both passion and assignment-driven. What is the correlation?

4. Review the fourteen traits that Smart Church Management suggests for effective leader interactions. Which ones represent your strengths? Your weaknesses?

42

Disconnected

This chapter reinforces many of my previously mentioned observations. It also exposes a major problem as it relates to American culture. I have watched as a gross disconnection continues to accelerate between our culture and the local church. This disconnection has been the cause for many to depart from faith communities. The dictionary gives several definitions for the word *disconnect*. All of them play into a heavy concern of mine as a pastor. Let's consider four of them:

1. To sever or interrupt the connection of or between
2. To detach
3. To withdraw into one's private world
4. A lack of communication or agreement

So what's my point? To fully explain my thoughts, consider a passage in Acts 2, which describes the lifestyle of Christians in the Early Church:

> They devoted themselves to the apostles'
> teaching and to fellowship, to the breaking of
> bread and to prayer. Everyone was filled with
> awe at the many wonders and signs performed
> by the apostles. All the believers were together

and had everything in common. They sold property and possessions to give to anyone who had need. Every day they continued to meet together in the temple courts. They broke bread in their homes and ate together with glad and sincere hearts, praising God and enjoying the favor of all the people. And the Lord added to their numbers daily those who were being saved. (2:42–47)

These early followers of Christ lived in community—not a commune—but in close and constant proximity to one another. They did life together! Their connection to Jesus Christ and one another made their unbelieving neighbors and friends take note, and because of their godly lifestyle and influence, others were finding new life in Christ on a daily basis (verse 47).

I do not wish to totally glorify this passage because, obviously, they had their problems too. We read about an issue regarding food distribution in Acts 6:1–6. As the number of disciples increased, tension developed between the Hellenistic Jews and the Hebraic Jews. The former group thought their widows were being treated unfairly because they were not receiving the same amount of food as the others. To resolve the infant Church's first recorded conflict, deacons were selected to assure proper oversight. They were selected to serve, not to rule. Still, the overriding theme of Acts 2:42–47 supports the idea that first-century Christians lived a life of "connection." They experienced strength in numbers and joy in fellowship. In short, they hung out together.

Back up a few verses to the Day of Pentecost (Acts 2:1–4). These 120 disciples of Jesus had been together in an upper room in Jerusalem for ten days. In all probability, they were together sixteen hours each day—praying, singing, repenting, celebrating communion, eating, and building relationships. Minus their sleep time, they were together a total of 160 hours. It would take almost two years of Sunday morning services today to equal their time spent together. Do we wonder why there's such a gross disconnection in most churches today?

Now, twenty-plus centuries later, believers in Christ often live separated and isolated lives. They attend church on Sundays and are likely not to see one another again until the following Sunday. Such a schedule cannot foster community and hinders the ability to experience perpetual, healthy relationships. Work hours, family activities, and life in general seem to prohibit them from spending time together. Of course, there are exceptions, but not many.

This trend has disconnected the lives of most Christians. Unless followers of Christ take the initiative to connect during the week, most live unto themselves, thus becoming separated from their source of spiritual growth and vitality. Many gradually leave their faith community for lesser pursuits. Disconnection spawns disillusionment.

Social media allows for a superficial type of connection but falls short of the three vital elements of effective communication as described in the life of Jesus Christ in 1 John 1:1. "That which was from the beginning, which we have *heard*, which we have *seen* with our eyes, which we have looked at and our hands have *touched*—this we proclaim concerning the Word of life (Jesus)." Effective communication results when we hear, see, and touch. That's why we need to regularly gather with other Christians. And this is where social media falls short. The early disciples functioned under these three communication dynamics. And their lives were woven together in a healthy way, which caused them to flourish and to grow exponentially. They impacted their "world" because they lived in connection with one another.

Just going to church on Sunday does not allow time for such connection. And yet, because of packed schedules and life necessities that keep Christians going in a myriad of directions, we continue to suffer from disconnection in today's fast-paced world. The Barna Research Group recently announced that not only was there disconnect in the lives of most Christians, but they offered two staggering statistics to support their research:

1. Regular church attendance is down. Four out of ten Christians in America are active churchgoers (or 38 percent).
2. Most people who attend church go 1.2 times each month. Oh my!

I'm greatly concerned with these trends. I've said it for years: "As goes the church, so goes the culture." We need a revival of connection! People often isolate themselves. The disintegration of family unity and values draws many into a self-isolating cocoon, where work and Netflix keep them hidden away. I'm concerned, if not frightened. Going to church one day, one service a week (if that) does not allow for lives to mesh. People can attend the same church for years and never truly know their fellow attendees. This truth is alarming. I understand that the cultures of Acts 2 versus today are miles apart, but I still say that no one flourishes spiritually when he lives as an island unto himself. It breaks my heart when I hear people say, "I don't feel part of the church," or "No one ever calls me or wonders how I'm doing," or "If I quit attending, no one would ever miss or even notice."

Guess what? Such comments represent the cold, harsh realities of a disconnected society. To further support my point, when I was a kid, we knew everyone on my street by name and at least a little bit about them. Today, it is not uncommon for people to never meet or talk to their neighbors—some who live only a few feet away! Again, I'm concerned. I don't have all the answers for this multifaceted issue, but let me offer the following starters to help you experience healthy community:

1. Accept Jesus Christ as your Savior.
2. Find a church home where Christ is honored and the Bible is preached.
3. Attend weekly services regularly. Arrive early. Hang around afterward!
4. Develop the gift of hospitality—open up your home for dinners, desserts, or if affordable, invite a family to eat out with you.
5. Get involved in a small group.
6. Quit expecting perfection, and for the love of God, quit picking everything apart.
7. Get rid of a potential consumer mentality and pour yourself into the life and service of your church family. It's not

about you when it comes to serving Jesus Christ; it's about others!

8. Don't compare large church to small church, worship with worship, or style with style.

9. Make concerted efforts to hang out with God's people during the weekdays.

10. Quit feeling sorry for yourself and quit expecting others to push through your self-isolation. You are responsible for your own disconnection.

11. Realize that ongoing connection with fellow believers will have to remain a priority in your life. You will need to remain intentional in your resolve to stay connected.

12. Disconnect with those things in your life that separate you from spiritual growth and development and connect with people who foster Christian community. Remember, "Bad company corrupts good character" (1 Cor. 15:33). Yes, you need to be salt and light in a dark world, but you cannot allow your convictions and need for connection to be determined by unbelievers. Do not be misled!

Christian friend, there are no easy answers to the problem of disconnection; however, staying home with the doors closed, curtains drawn, lights dimmed, TV blasting, and pity parties in full swing is not the solution. Spiritually speaking, self-isolation fosters a slow spiritual decline. Determine today to stay connected to the very life source that led you to salvation.

Questions to Ponder

1. Have you ever felt disconnected from your local church? What responsibility do you assume?

2. What steps did you take to remedy your feelings?

3. What are the three vital elements to effective communication?

4. Compare Acts 2:42–47 to church life in the United States today. What can Christians do to become reconnected?

43

For This Cause

In today's world, causes are not in short supply: health care reform, election reform, civil rights, climate change, immigration, animal cruelty, the homeless, vaccinations, Save the Whale, Save the Dolphins, save "whatever," home churches, and countless others. Cause-oriented and cause-driven people fill Facebook posts. Conversations in general center around those causes near and dear to us. Inherently, there is nothing wrong with this; however, let me sound a warning, especially to all professing Christians.

God's people need to remember that one cause overrides all others: the cause of Jesus Christ. Even in the church people tend to elevate causes that fall into a nonessential category. Worship styles, song selections, preaching series, coffee bars in church, sound volume, dress codes, and other issues capture the attention of churchgoers, often "CAUSing" division and unrest. I'm continually amazed at how the enemy successfully maneuvers godly people to focus on lesser pursuits. Believe me, a lot of issues beckon for my attention; however, I'm determined to remain very selective to what I give my time and energy. My wife often cautions me to be careful what I give brain space to! Please give the following questions/comments your careful attention:

1. If you feel strongly about a specific cause, avoid becoming disagreeable in the face of disagreements.

2. Ask yourself, "Does my approach need to be altered?" "Am I building bridges or walls?" "Have I come across mean-spirited, even hateful?" Christians, especially, have to consider how they're perceived.

3. Am I adhering to the "good-better-best" principle in my life? Always remember, good and better causes abound. But are you giving your life to those things close to the heart of God? In other words, is what you're doing cause-worthy?

4. Do you understand that some causes are best confronted through fervent prayer? The infamous quote, "The only thing necessary for the triumph of evil is for good men to do nothing" has merit, but be careful saint that you devote your life to those things that come alongside the local church, not steal you away to lesser pursuits.

5. The apostle Paul makes it clear to believers that one cause supersedes all others: "For this cause (reason), I Paul, a prisoner of Jesus Christ" (Eph. 3:1). Paul's reason for living was to carry the life-changing Gospel to the Gentile world. I may be splitting hairs, but it concerns me when Christ followers spend their time and energy never affecting positive change, end their days tired and frustrated, and live with an antagonistic mind-set. Positive, long-term change seldom, if ever, comes when divisive, at times violent confrontational hearts demand their way. Yes, Paul was at times confrontational but always love-driven.

He writes in 2 Corinthians 5:14, "The love of Christ constrains (compels) me." Another translation says, "The love of Christ drives me…" Love for the lost was his motivating force! We may embrace a mind-set where personal opinion is king; however, the downside to this liberty is mishandling our approach to those issues we feel so strongly about. Talking down to people, degrading comments, and unkind words never achieve righteous outcomes. It concerns me that the Church in many sectors of society is known more for what we're against than what we're for. Do we walk in agape love—God's love?

We, the Church, are stewards of the greatest cause known to mankind. "Jesus Christ came into the world to save sinners" (1 Tim. 1:15). Your greatest privilege as a believer in Jesus is to tell anyone and everyone who will listen! When people think of you, do they appreciate your Christ-likeness, or do they equate you with controversy and unrest? Are you known for sporting causes that put those around you on edge? Remember what Paul wrote to the young preacher Timothy:

> But refuse foolish and ignorant speculations, knowing that they produce quarrels. The Lord's bondservant must not be quarrelsome, but be kind to all, able to teach, patient when wronged, with gentleness correcting those who are in opposition, if perhaps God may grant them repentance leading to the knowledge of the truth. (2 Tim. 2:23–25)

Witness not only with your words, but with your lifestyle, your actions, and your attitudes. If Jesus tells you to speak out against a given cause, then bleed love and brokenness! And make sure your primary cause—Jesus Christ—is first and foremost.

Filter every cause through the Cross. Weigh the temporary against the eternal and make sure your highest goal is to point others to the saving knowledge of Jesus Christ. Proverbs 11:30 says, "The fruit of the righteous is a tree of life, and he who wins souls is wise." The preacher encourages us to use our righteous influence to touch and change our surroundings. He reminds us there's our way, then God's way of doing things. Follow the way of wisdom! Sadly, many causes are picked up by those who employ counterproductive methods.

Finally, and you had to know this was coming! When lesser causes pull individuals and their families away from the local church, the enemy leads them into a "no-impact zone" of life. Again, the enemy knows how to drive cause-oriented people away from the house of God, and when he does their lives become earmarked by what they don't like, what they disagree with or a struggle to find and hold sustainable relationships. Such causes often distract well-meaning people to never discuss the saving Gospel with those who need the Lord.

Did you read about the man in Tennessee who left his dog five million dollars in his will? It's true! Headlines were clear: "Border collie becomes millionaire after man leaves $5 million to his pet." The article read in part, "Lula, an 8-year-old border collie must be one of the richest dogs in the world, after her 84 year-old owner named her as a beneficiary in his will." I would definitely say that dog was man's best friend!

However, his cause, to say the least, is eccentric by most standards. Perhaps a gift of that magnitude would be understood if given to the Animal Protective League (APL). For sure! But not just one dog. We might say his cause was short-sighted. Misdirected zeal perhaps leads many to take on causes that produce little effect and steal wasted energy and time away from matters that really matter in the scheme of productive living! Christians, especially, are called upon to make a difference in their sphere of influence. Local churches provide opportunities for God's people to make a difference in their community. Loving people into the kingdom of God sure beats shadow boxing—wasting time taking a swing at causes that make no difference in the long run, or those causes one cannot change in a thousand lifetimes. People who become disengaged from local churches to pursue outside causes are like the man and his dog: well-meaning and even love-driven, but failing to realize they need to maximize their efforts on eternal rather than temporal issues. In other words, provide for the daily needs of the dog over his lifetime, but remember, there are greater causes that produce fruits of righteousness and more widespread results.

Questions to Ponder

1. To what cause(s) have you devoted your life?

2. Does this chapter challenge you to rethink your future causes?

3. Have you ever got caught up in a cause that you realized later was time consuming and energy draining, but less than satisfying?

4. Talk to your pastor. What can you do to help move the cause of Jesus Christ forward through your church?

44

Compel, Not Repel

$\mathscr{I}$ realize we have to live according to good doctrine. Right doctrine leads to right living. Let me define the word *doctrine* in case I'm not clear. Doctrine is a system of belief regarding a specific biblical topic. For example, the rapture of the Church is an eschatological doctrine that finds its support by grouping all end time Scriptures together, and coming up with a solid biblical teaching. The "catching away" of the Church is the doctrine. My resolve to daily live close to the Lord is my response to this belief. "And all who have this eager expectation will keep themselves pure, just as he is pure" (1 John 3:3).

I believe Christians should know what they believe, why they believe it and who they believe. Paul E. Little's timeless trilogy remains a must read for all who love the Lord and their local church. And certainly, a general understanding of the entire Bible is necessary in order to live a balanced spiritual life. However, I am saddened by believers who use what they hold dear to literally bring offense and division to the body of Christ.

I appreciate all the streams of true Christian endeavor. All who recognize Christ as the only Son of God, virgin born, crucified, dead and buried, risen again, and the only way to God are my brothers and sisters. We will share heaven! I've come to understand that I can believe something not quite scripturally accurate and still go to heaven. If truth be told, we all do! We do, however, have to hold true to the essentials of our faith. We are ever-learning about the wonderful mystery of "Christ in us, the hope of glory" (Col. 1:27).

While studying 1 Corinthians 13, one particular word caught my attention. It was Paul's use of *three* in verse 13. "And now abides faith, hope, love, these three, but the greatest of these is love." Tagged on the end of this infamous wedding passage, the apostle summarizes the essence of Christian doctrine and everyday living. I marvel at other uses of "three" in the Bible. Here are a few more examples:

1. Israel has three patriarchs: Abraham, Isaac, and Jacob.
2. Jonah was in the whale for three days.
3. God appeared to Abraham and Sarah as three persons.
4. Isaiah says that God is three times holy.
5. The wise men brought three gifts to Jesus: gold, frankincense, and myrrh.
6. Jesus stayed forty days in the wilderness and was tempted three times.
7. Three men witnessed Jesus's Transfiguration: Peter, James, and John.
8. Peter denied Jesus three times.
9. Jesus was crucified on the third hour (9:00 a.m.) and died on the ninth hour (3:00 p.m.).
10. Jesus was in the tomb three days.

So the number 3 in the Bible signifies the idea of harmony or wholeness. There are countless other examples. That's why every good story has a beginning, middle, and end. And most striking of all, we worship God the Father, God the Son, and God the Holy Spirit—the three in One! Pause this very moment and give him praise!

While Paul often emphasized faith and hope in his letters, the overriding theme of his life and ministry was love. I discovered many years ago that people can believe right doctrine, but if love is not the motivating force behind what they believe, they render their message null and void. More things are caught in the Christian life than taught! Paul compared the absence of love to "sounding brass and a tinkling cymbal" (verse 1). All of us probably have known

Christians who felt the need to protect their church's "pet doctrine" at the expense of coming across exclusive or even "better than."

In chapter 11, I talk about every church having an assignment. I have watched both churches and pastors embrace an exclusive mind-set, where they filtered everything they preached and taught through the lens of one particular doctrine. In other words, their ministry became defined by their love for a specific area of teaching. Notwithstanding of course, local churches must answer the question, "What are we supposed to do in our community? What's our assignment?"

And I believe we can all agree the Church's (big *C*) primary role is to help those who are far from God find new life in Jesus Christ. The mission of any local church (little *c*) is twofold: to win the lost to Christ and subsequently make disciples. Matthew 28:19 remains our mandate: "Go, and teach all nations, baptizing them in the name of the Father, and the Son, and the Holy Spirit." We dare not subvert the Great Commission—winning the lost. Local churches are given the task to take as many from their community to heaven as they possibly can. Heaven will be largely populated due to the faithful witness of local churches that presented the saving Gospel of Jesus Christ. How I thank the Lord for a small church in my community that preached Jesus! I'm so thankful their emphasis was salvation and discipleship!

I also discussed primary versus secondary assignments given to local churches and parachurch ministries. First, let me say that it is always counterproductive for churches to judge and verbally undermine one another. Using the pulpit to openly bash or malign another church provides the enemy necessary fodder to divide the work of God. The kingdom of God always suffers reproach when believers are thrown into confusion and a competitive mind-set. We need to constantly remember that we are not in competition with other churches; we are in a battle for the souls of men. To undermine other churches in a given community is to operate under demonic principle. We aid and abet the enemy when we participate in spiritual smear campaigns. When will we learn that to disagree never gives us the green light to become disagreeable? Let's remember who our real enemy is.

If COVID-19 did anything for me, it required me to search the deep recesses of my heart to identify those things in my life that really matter. And then to discard those areas that only weigh me down and bring unnecessary stress in my life. Strife, confusion, and self-induced stress become harsh taskmasters. What I believe really does impact how I feel, how I view the kingdom of God, how I treat other people, and cements my identity to a local church.

We hear a lot today about ministry that lodges outside of local church expression. Let me explain the difference between church and parachurch ministry. *Para* means to come alongside, so parachurch groups are Christian faith-based organizations that usually carry out their mission independent of church oversight. They serve the local church and fulfill the Great Commission at her side. Examples of parachurch groups would be Campus Crusade for Christ, Master's Commission, Teen Challenge, Alpha Course, Christian Motorcyclist Association, Child Evangelism Fellowship, Promise Keepers, and countless other Christ-honoring ministries. Thank God for the many parachurch groups that reinforce what local churches do. It's so wonderful when God's people unite under parachurch banners, although some of them may not completely line up with our preferred doctrinal positions. As long as their heart for souls is center stage, and Gospel essentials are held up without compromise, we have an ally in the kingdom.

Church doctrine that separates and builds walls among the people of God should be a cause for concern. None of us hold a corner on the market when it comes to embracing total truth. I constantly cry out for wisdom as it pertains to effectively communicating the Gospel. The preacher said it this way: "Wisdom cries aloud in the street, in the market she raises her voice; at the head of the noisy streets she cries out; at the entrance of the city gates she speaks" (Prov. 1:20–21). Have you ever wondered why we conduct our church services like we do? Is it possible that we forget our intended audience? Do we assume that those who enter our doors know what's going on? Do they know what to expect? Do we communicate our reason for being with clarity, so as to avoid confusion? Yes, what we believe is important, but if we don't effectively communicate with unbelievers, we can perhaps push them away. Doctrine not explained may harm instead of bringing redemptive life to people. Think about it!

The local church is called upon to present a clearly understood presentation of the Gospel. Many leaders today hear the term "balanced ministry" and think "compromise." And yet, Paul told the believers in Corinth that imbalanced doctrine—in this case spiritual gifts—might cause outsiders to ask, "Are you all mad?" (verse 23). Our mandate from the apostle is that "things be done decently and in order" (verse 40). While those in the church may understand, those outside may literally be repelled instead of compelled! Every local church needs to have a compelling outreach, and never pride itself on being repelling for Jesus's sake. "Go out into the highways and along the hedges, and *compel* them to come in, so that My house may be filled" (Luke 14:23). Doctrine should never set us apart in a weird way, but enhance the assignment God has placed upon us.

Local churches that constantly emphasize the gifts of the Holy Spirit, the prophetic, end-time events, healing, prosperity, miracles, signs, and wonders, are not more spiritual than other churches. I believe they're more accountable! And Christians who embrace these wonderful biblical truths must walk in humility, seeking opportunities to walk out the life of Jesus in such a way that attracts people, not pushes them away, or makes them feel uncomfortable, or God forbid, like second-class Christians. Any church that chooses to emphasize one specific doctrine and to become defined by that doctrine negates the whole of Scripture. Family ministry is likely not to happen in these churches, which limits their outreach capabilities. Their overemphasis may be their undoing. My friend, churches today need to present the whole counsel of God. An overemphasis on one major doctrine automatically excludes a large portion of people in a given community from attending that church. Let's get back to balanced biblical preaching that draws from the entire canon of Scripture. This is not compromise; it promotes essential Christian living! Could it be that some churches have embraced a parachurch assignment? I think so!

Doctrinal overemphasis creates two expressions: experiential and emotionally driven Christians, or those who downplay emotion at any level, thus hindering supernatural intervention and assigning it solely to the pages of the Bible. Both expressions constitute extremes. God is still touching this earth with his presence. Yes, seek him daily in his Word. Yes, trust that he wants to intervene in the affairs of your life. But never present the Christian experience as weird or something exclusive and out of reach. "But you are *a chosen race, a royal priesthood, a holy nation, a people for God's own possession*, so that you may proclaim the excellencies of Him who has called you out of darkness into his marvelous light" (1 Pet. 2:9). God's desire for every local church is that it proclaims a Gospel message that issues a call for the salvation of the lost.

I think we forget our target audience—those far from God. It's hard to respond to Gospel claims above the noise of "sounding brass and tinkling cymbals." If what we believe and practice as Christians unsettles unbelievers, then we may need to rethink our communication strategies. I agree that any church ministry that excludes the moving of the Spirit runs the risk of becoming rote and lifeless. But I also agree that until local churches become more interested in winning the lost than touting their exclusive doctrines, they may place the Great Commission in jeopardy. I heard a radio preacher say, "We may be small in number, but we're powerful in the Spirit." I believe he was saying that same thing five years ago. Gray heads prevail! How sad.

Local church ministry that supports an "us four and no more"—exclusivistic—mind-set has lost its reason for being. Local churches that forget the necessity of momentum and the power of influence most always fade into oblivion and remain the best kept secret in their community. Remember, doctrine—what we believe and hold dear—must point others to the saving grace of Jesus. If doctrine becomes an end in itself, local churches will stalemate and become elite Christian sub-communities instead of life-giving venues. Your community deserves opportunities to experience the life of Jesus, not imbalanced, overemphasized indoctrination. Ask the Holy Spirit how to more clearly communicate earth's greatest message. While good doctrine is important, a clear presentation will more likely bring perpetuity to local churches. Those far from God need to see a church united instead of a church divided due to doctrinal malfeasance.

When our stream of Christian endeavor minimizes our capacity to win the lost to Christ and make disciples, we probably need to rethink our approach. Communication that misses its intended mark must be redirected in a way that propels the Gospel forward in each community. Local churches hold the key to their community's future. May God help us communicate the essence of the Gospel, not our particular "flavor." For example, most Pentecostal Christians highlight speaking in tongues as the evidence that one has become Spirit-filled. My point here is not to debate this teaching, but only to say that Acts 1:8, the key verse of this historical book reminds us, "You shall receive power, after the Holy Spirit comes upon you, and you shall be witnesses." If we're not careful, tongues many times become elevated above the essence of the encounter itself. Luke tells us the essence of the Spirit baptism is "power."

As a lifelong Pentecostal, I've watched as many emphasize the evidence (tongues) over the essence and, frankly, take the experience to a level of unnecessary confusion. I constantly counsel individuals to "seek Jesus, not tongues." Where tongues are billboarded, some who seek this wonderful work of grace need always to remember that it is the "Spirit who gives the utterance" (2:4). Human ingenuity has no place in this experience. People need not be prodded, assisted, or coached to receive what only a yielded, praising vessel can receive! Oh, how I long for a recall of solid teaching when it comes to the Spirit baptism!

I see church signs that read: "*KJV* Only." "Have you received the Holy Ghost since you believed?" "Turn or Burn," "We are Full Gospel," "Get Right or Get Left," and others too painful to list; and I ask, "Do we really feel that those far from God are going to be drawn to our house of worship?" These slogans may be cute, but they fall short in the understanding department! I've been in the faith for fifty years, and I'm not completely sure what some of those slogans mean. Why would unbelievers be attracted to local churches by these unclear communications? Again, such evangelistic slogans are "churchy" but not relevant.

May what we believe and what we communicate reflect the beauty of Jesus over having to always scratch our particular religious itch! Now that I've made some of you mad, some wanting to hang me in effigy for my perceived compromises, and others praying for my salvation, let's move on to money matters, yet another reason people leave local churches!

Questions to Ponder

1. Can you define the term *doctrine?*

2. Why is it important that we embrace right doctrine?

3. What happens when churches solely espouse one main doctrine?

4. One translation uses the phrase, "We are a peculiar people." Does this mean "weird"?

5. An overemphasis on one major doctrine can lead to exclusive, unapproachable ministry. Do you understand why?

45

Money, Money, Money

I purposely saved this topic for last. And this I believe to be proven, not speculative! One of the biggest indictments leveled against local churches is their alleged overemphasis on money. Televangelists, the rise of megachurches, and Christian ministries in general have been targeted by those who understand in part only. It takes money to operate homes, schools, businesses, government offices, restaurants, etc. And of course, it takes money to operate churches. I have never understood why some criticize churches for needing money. This kind of thinking is faulty. It is incongruous. The world says, "Put your money where your mouth is." God asks us to put our money where our heart is. What I love, what I value, I finance. Look at my checkbook entries, and you will know what I hold dear. Because I believe in the mission of the Christ-honoring local church, I gladly support it. I have said for years, "To not regularly attend and give my finances is my vote to close the doors." This remains my firm conviction.

Has there been financial abuse in churches? For sure! It would be ridiculous to deny such a claim. Unfortunately, nationally known ministers are targeted by yellow journalists in attempts to discredit their integrity. John Q. Public then builds his case against alleged church over-indulgence. Should some ministers live more modestly to help downplay some of the many attacks leveled against lavish lifestyles? I think it would be wise. And can we quit emphatically telling people that a premiere sign of spirituality is accumulated wealth? I don't adhere to the "keep 'em poor, keep 'em, humble," mind-set, but I agree that sometimes the church tends to operate in extremes. When you keep me poor, you keep me frustrated! Local churches, of course, need to take care of their pastors in a more than generous manner; however, they need not present a community image that relays the wrong message.

To be fair, abuse can be found in every home, institution, and organization when it comes to finances. The mishandling of money is a sad reality, and one that certainly needs to be corrected at all costs! We must take measures to ensure the proper collection and disbursement of monies entrusted to us. Local churches should strive to protect their financial integrity. The Internal Revenue Service is our friend, not our enemy. It is good to give an account! Open books and full disclosure bring honor to the Lord and keep all of us righteously accountable.

A lot of churches teach on tithing and encourage their constituency to honor the Lord with the first 10 percent of their income. Those who refuse to at least consider God's way of financing the kingdom perhaps need to look within. Leaving a church over giving clearly reveals a negative heart condition. Again, let me reiterate: Our money follows our heart, our priorities. Tithing reminds us that everything we have belongs to God and keeps our affections turned toward eternal, not earthly things. We simply steward what God gives us! Tithing is mentioned in both the Old and New Testament. In the Old Testament, nowhere do we see it taught more poignantly than in Malachi 3:8–11.

> Will a man rob God? Yet you are robbing me! But you say, "How have we robbed you?" In tithes and offerings. "You are cursed with a curse, for you are robbing Me, the whole nation of you!" Bring the whole tithe into the storehouse, so that there may be food in My house, and test Me now in this,' says the Lord of hosts, "If I will not open for you the windows of heaven and pour out for you a blessing until it overflows.

> Then I will rebuke the devourer for you, so that
> it will not destroy the fruits of the ground; nor
> will your vine in the field cast its grapes," says the
> Lord of hosts.

May I direct your attention away from what you've done to what God does? He says in verse 11, "I will rebuke the devourer." I must be honest and admit that I, too, have wrestled with this passage of Scripture. In my opinion, I think that perhaps we have misapplied what the minor prophet is really saying.

Early in our marriage, my wife and I suffered the loss of earthly possessions and a good credit score due to financial lack in our home. However, because I believe the credit industry in this country operates according to boorish principles, maintaining a high credit score is not the goal of my life. It may give me lower interest rates when I go to finance a home or car, but it is not an idol in my life. That's not to say we shouldn't pay our bills on time; it simply overrides the condemnation, shame, and guilt the credit industry places upon us when, for reasons beyond our control, we're not able to meet our financial obligations in a timely manner.

Luke 6:38 remains another verse that also throws earnest believers into a quandary. "Give, and it shall be given unto you; good measure pressed down, and shaken together, and running over, shall men give into your bosom. For with the same measure you give out, it shall be given back to you." I refuse to defend God in either one of these verses. They appear to be ironclad principles, but sometimes, things happen to us in life that beckon us to reconsider the deeper messages of these verses. Let's rightfully divide the Word!

Malachi 3 was written to the nation of Israel who had become arrogant and rebellious toward God. Their open defiance took them from blessings to curses. In Luke 6:38, Jesus is not talking about money. If you look at verse 37, you find that the subject of his discourse is judging and criticizing others. When we judge and criticize others, it comes back to us many times over—always more severely.

In Malachi, the prophet does not suggest that tithing and giving offerings ensures a never-ending supply of money or a problem-free financial existence. I've seen people who faithfully tithed and then mishandled the remaining 90 percent. Psalm 23:1 reminds us that, "The Lord is our shepherd, and we shall not lack" (what we need). However, I think we need to redefine needs versus wants. In the original Hebrew, the words, "There shall not be room enough to receive it" do not appear in the original manuscripts (Mal. 3:10). This possibility certainly confuses those who wrestle with greed and get-rich-quick schemes.

The real emphasis lies in verse 11: "And I will rebuke the devourer for your sakes." Some years ago, the Lord gave me insight into this verse: If a dog attacks you, and sinks his teeth into your leg, he may badly hurt you, but he can't wholly devour you. In the same way, if the devourer (Satan) tries to devour you, God will not let him completely destroy you. You may suffer loss, but you still come out on top! First Peter 5:8 it says, "Be of sober spirit, be on the alert. Your adversary, the devil, prowls around like a roaring lion, seeking someone to devour."

Personally, I tire of the imbalanced preaching I hear regarding the giving of tithes and offerings. I'm upset with the crowd who teaches that God blesses according to how much we give. In other words, the size and amount of your blessings are determined by how much you give. Our God is not a slot machine! While I believe the Bible supports tithing—the giving of 10 percent of our income—I equally believe that God looks at the motivation behind giving. Second Corinthians 9 is the New Testament correlation to Malachi 3. Paul says, "God loves a cheerful giver" (verse 7).

I believe we should give generously and cheerfully. I believe we should give not because we have to, but because we love Christ! I believe we should give out of our "first fruits." Attitude when we give is always more important than the amount we give. Obedience always follows love! Simply stated, I believe that God honors giving. He gives us resources to use and invest for him. Paul uses the illustration of seeds to explain that the resources God gives us are not to be hidden, foolishly devoured or thrown away, but cultivated in order to produce more crops. When we invest what God has given us in his work, he will provide us with even more to give. We all understand that we won't reap if we don't sow. If we plow and don't plant, we won't reap! I've said it many times: "If we'll seek God's face, he will release what's in his hands!" God loves to bless his people!

However, along with finances, Paul emphasizes spiritual rewards for those who give generously to God's work. We should not expect to become wealthy through giving. Those who receive our gifts will be helped, will praise God, and will pray for us. As we bless others, we are blessed! I believe that giving to God does place a protective bond around our lives. However, we live in a world where inequities abound. Many things that happen to us in life are unfair. The important thing, and I believe the overriding principle for believers to remember, is that giving to God assures that we will not be "devoured."

People of all ages, races, and descriptions suffer loss of properties and possessions every day. But God still causes them to triumph! Obviously, losing a house or a job is a very heart-rending, difficult thing. However, there are worse things that can happen to a believer. During times of loss, I believe we have to look to God for a deeper interpretation of the facts, and for his grace, which sustains us even in the darkest of times.

If we compare our plight to other believers, we may very well become discouraged and perhaps bitter. Asking "why" during times of loss is perfectly okay; however, dwelling on the apparent inequity may cause us to stumble in our faith. I believe in the sovereignty of God, which says to me, that no matter what may happen in my life, Jesus is still Lord, and he will provide a way of escape. Remember, we don't have to give our money to the Lord's work, we get to! The kingdom of God as expressed through the local church is earth's greatest enterprise. Please don't allow money to blind you from seeing God's heart in matters of giving. Any investments you make during offering times reap benefits that are out of this world! You can only draw on deposits made in your chosen bank. Similarly, when you give to God's work, you will always have deposits from which to draw.

Being a pastor, I perhaps used this platform to defend the local church's right and privilege to receive tithes and offerings. And I humbly ask those who have chosen to embrace misguided thinking and even accusations against this practice to reconsider their ways. I join with the prophet Haggai who, in his day, addressed wide-scale neglect against the house of the Lord with these words: "Now therefore, thus says the Lord of hosts, 'Consider your ways! You have sown much, but harvest little; you eat, but there is not enough to be satisfied; you drink, but there is not enough to become drunk; you put on clothing, but no one is warm enough; and he who earns, earns wages to put into a purse with holes'" (1:5–6). Again, the Lord says in verse 7, "Consider your ways!" What was the Lord's indictment? The people lived in nice homes while the temple lay in ruin. The Lord has always placed a high premium on his house. The underlying principle here is that if we take care of God's house, he will take care of ours!

Don't throw the baby out with the dirty bathwater. For every poor example in the local church, there are hundreds, if not thousands, of God-fearing, Christ-loving, Spirit-led men and women who are doing it right in terms of their finances and the church's finances. These are unsung heroes who often make great personal financial sacrifices to lead local churches.

I understand my bias, and ask all those who love and support their local church to join me in making sure that we lead in a way pleasing to the Lord, with heaven's backing.

Questions to Ponder

1. Why do you think some people get hung up on giving tithes and offerings but are willing to spend inordinate amounts of money on other interests?

2. In your opinion, why is it prudent for ministers to guard their fiducial lifestyle choices?

3. Does paying tithes and offerings guarantee problem-free money matters?

A Sad Story

$\mathcal{A}$ criticism sometimes leveled against me is that I place too much emphasis on going to church, of being part of a church family. When recently asking the Lord if my dogmatic opinion needed altering, my wife shared a sad story with me. A story I've heard repeated many times throughout my ministry. And a story that reinforced my already strong conviction.

A couple who once regularly attended the services of their church, who held key leadership roles and who personally won many of their family and friends to the Lord, is now in the process of getting a divorce. They raised their three children in church but, in recent years, met with offenses that cut them to their very core. They subsequently left their beloved church after many years of active service. Today, they are angry and bitter. Their once strong faith, now compromised, wants nothing to do with "church." It seems the enemy has scored yet another victory.

Hell, fast and furiously, targets those who absent themselves from the house of God. An entire family, once a vital part of a local church, now faces untold heartache and loss—all alone. When individuals come out from under the protective custody of the local church, they open themselves up to the destructive devices of the enemy and become spiritual casualties. And God forbid that unwise church leaders bear the responsibility for creating such tragic scenarios.

I'm convinced more than ever the local church remains God's saving and keeping grace for people everywhere. *Monday Morning Preacher*, although not an exhaustive treatment on why people come and go, proves again that the local church, despite its apparent flaws, is worth fighting for. The author prays that pastors, former pastors, and other church leaders everywhere will rise up in the power of the Holy Spirit to ensure the success of their faith community we call the Church. "May there be fewer casualties! In Jesus's name. Amen."

A Final Thought

In conclusion, let me say it again: The local church is a family. And like all families, there come times of disagreement, unkind words, and offenses. Because we are God's people and because we desire to safeguard God's reputation in our lives and church family, we readily forgive one another! The home and the local church are laboratories where our faith is practiced and put to the test. May we tenaciously hold to those truths that unite us as brothers and sisters and determine to stem the tide of those who leave local churches Our communities and surrounding areas are watching. We have what they need—a vibrant witness of saving grace and a place to call "home." We must protect it!

References

Introduction

Earls, Aaron, "Majority of American Churches Fall Below 100 in Worship Attendance," February 14, 2016. Lifeway Research.

Hartford Institute for Religious Research, "Megachurches in the United States," November 26, 2018

Pastoral Care, Inc.

Inc.com/statistics/clarification-on-statistics/

Pastoral Care, Inc, Oknulgee, Oklahoma, "Clarification and Discussion Concerning Our Statistics," 2020

The Big Question

Vankbevering, Dr. Joe, "100-Year-Old Vision Conveys Sobering Warning to the Church." *Charisma Leader*, March 13, 2013

When It's All Said and Done

Mahatma Gandhi, "Quotable Quotes." goodreads.com.

Peterson, Paul, "Why Does the Church Exist?" paulpetersonlive.com.

Never the Same Again

Gillespie, Claire, *Explore Health*, "What are Comorbidities—and How Do They Affect COVID-19? Here's What Experts Say," February 17, 2021.

Zuckerman, Arthur, *CompareCamp Research Team*. "60 Church Attendance Statistics: 2020/2021 Data, Trends and Predictions."

The Church Goes to Church

Eskenazi, Tamara Cohn, *Bible Odyssey*, "The Destruction and Reconstruction of the Temple," March 12, 2021
Acreman, Thomas, *Classic History*, "Roman Emperor Constantine's Conversion to Christianity," January 14, 2020.
Breeden, Adam and Auralein, *New York Times*, "Fire Mauls Beloved Notre Dame Cathedral in Paris," April 15, 2019.

More Miss Than Hit

Benjamin, Ronna, "The Art of Absquatulating: Is it OK to Leave a Party Without Saying Goodbye?" September 20, 2016.

Doubting the Goodness of God

en.wickipedia.org>wild>Effects_of_Hurricane_Laura.2020California Wildfires.
en.wickipedia.org/wiki/2020_

Virtual Church

Statistics-prove-the-obvious-the-internet-is-for-porn.

All Aboard?

History.com, "A Miraculous Home Run Wins the Pennant for the NY Giants."

No Lead-In Material

Dobbins, Richard D., *Invisible Imprint: What Others Feel When in Your Presence*, February 19, 2002.

Talking Trash

Intrater, Keith, *Covenant Relationships: A Handbook for Integrity and Loyalty*, Destiny Image Publishers, 2016.

When Johnny Can't Read

Flesch, Rudolph, *Why Johnny Can't Read: And What You Can Do About It*, Harper and Brothers, 1955.
Flesch, Rudolph, *Why Johnny Still Can't Read: A New Look at the Scandal of Our Schools*, Harper Collins, 1983.
TIME Magazine, "Why Johnny Can't/Can Read," August 15, 1955.

Times Have Changed

National Congregational Study Survey, https://www.beaconjournal.com>local>>2020/08/22
Russell, Taylor Billings, Center for Analytical, Research and Data (CARD), "Are 10,000 Churches Closing Every Year?"
Smith, Greg, "So What Faith," 2021.
Santayana, George, inspiringquotes.us.

Emotional Residue

Herbert, Dr. Claudia, "Getting Stuck in Your Trauma," Oxford Development Centre, Center for Trauma Healing and Growth.
https://www.dmarikovanen.co.uk>healing_mother_wounds
https://www.dmarikovanen.co.uk>healing_father_wounds

A Higher Standard

Duran, Eduardo, *Healing the Soul Wound: Counseling with America*, Teachers College Press, 2019.
Emerge Ministries, Akron, Ohio 44313 (330)867-5603.

Trust Your Leader

Dobbins, Dr. Richard, *Christian Counseling Course*, "Healing of the Mind," YouTube, August 21, 2010.

Yates, Dr. Harry and Joanne Cash Yates, *Nashville Cowboy Church Broadcast*, ℅ Landmark Communications Group, 116 West Rockwood Street, Rockwood, Tennessee 37854.

The Heart of Worship

Redman, Matt, "The Heart of Worship" (The Heart of Worship story behind the song and reflections on listening to 20 years of modern worship), March 27, 2019.

McLuhan, Marshall, *Understanding Media: The Extension of Man*, "The Medium is the Message," McGraw Hill Education, 1964.

Church Hoppers

"The Apostle's Creed," Synod of Milan, AD 390.

The Great Falling Away

Artesona, Eva, Producer, "The Storming of the U.S. Capitol," BBC News, January 13, 2021.

Comparisons

Dobbins, Dr. Richard Dobbins, Founder and President, Dr. Richard D. Dobbins Ministries, Inc., Marriage Seminars.

The Ten Suggestions

Horowitz, Juliana M., "Marriage and Cohabitation in the U.S.," Pew Research Center.

Noble, Jason, *Des Moines Register*, "Reality Fact Check: Fact Check," Guttmacher Institute, March 17, 2015.

Wilkerson, David, "A Call to Anguish," SermonIndex.net (Promoting Genuine Biblical Revival).

Keeping Score

Dobbins, Dr. Richard D. Dobbins, *The Institute for Pastoral Counseling*, "The Healing of the Universe" (Course 102).
Ryle, J. C., "Justification, Grace Gems! A Treasury of Ageless Devotional Writings."

Both Made and Born

Maxwell, John, "Are You Really Leading, or are You Just Taking a Walk?" johnmaxwell.com, August 7, 2012.
Maxwell, John, "A Leader is One Who Knows the Way, Goes the Way, Shows the Way," johnmaxwell.com, May 23, 2019.
Smart Church Management, "14 Traits of Effective Leadership," September 19, 2018.

Compel, Not Repel

Little, Paul E., *Know Why You Believe*, InterVarsity Press, February 2000
Little, Paul E., *Know What You Believe*, Cook, David C., January 2005
Little, Paul E., *Know Who You Believe*, InterVarsity Press, February 2008

About the Author

$\mathcal{R}$oger Loomis graduated from Evangel University, later doing postgraduate work at Liberty University. He and his wife, Lori, have pastored six churches in North Carolina, Alabama, and Ohio respectively. They founded and now pastor Hope Community, a nondenominational church, located in Jefferson, Ohio. The Loomis's are ordained with the Assemblies of God International Fellowship (E4 Ministry Network), headquartered in San Diego, California. *Monday Morning Preacher* is a learning composite of their forty-three years of co-pastoring.